AF342250

Oriental Gardens
in America

A Visitor's Guide

Oriental Gardens in America

A Visitor's Guide

by Dorothy Loa McFadden

Photos by James L. McFadden,
Dorothy Loa McFadden, & Others

DOUGLAS-WEST PUBLISHERS, INC.   LOS ANGELES, CALIFORNIA

A Note from the Author

Visiting gardens has long been a favorite pastime of my husband and myself. On frequent business trips to other countries, we devote many leisure hours to photographing historic and memorable places. When in need of relaxation, we search out a quiet lovely garden where we may enjoy an interval of peacefulness away from the hustle and stress of city life. Gardens are very important to us, and in recent years writing about them has become a delightful and fulfilling avocation.

The stories behind gardens have always fascinated us. There is a strong common bond between all lovers of gardens which usually makes for instant friendship. Consequently, I have been privileged to learn about a great many public as well as private gardens and "how they grew," and to enjoy the hospitality of garden owners in many parts of the world.

I am deeply indebted to them and to many other friends for their invaluable assistance in bringing together in one volume this first complete guide to Oriental gardens in America; for it was the interest of American gardeners and designers which prompted me to undertake this demanding but pleasurable task.

I wish to express my gratitude to the many chambers of commerce for their generous and often time-consuming assistance, with a special tribute to Sister Cities of Japan, through Mr. Will Hippen, Jr., Honorary Consul General of Japan at San Diego, which is a Sister City. I am grateful also to the Sister City Society of San Diego for nationwide listings of Oriental gardens, and to

Amy Wormser for the use of her remarkable collection of garden books.

Special thanks must surely go to Professor Koichi Kawana, well-known landscape architect, and Architectural Associate at the University of California, Los Angeles; to Dr. H. Carroll Parish, former Dean at U.C.L.A. for verifying Japanese information; and to Dr. S. M. Randhawa, Vice Chancellor of Punjab Agricultural University in India. My sincere gratitude to Dr. Massoud Simnad who generously permitted the use of excerpts from *The Persian Garden: Its Origin and Development,* a treasured work written by his nephew, Mohammad Gheissari.

Heartfelt thanks to members of my family: my granddaughter Susan J. McFadden, who researched gardens for me while teaching in Taiwan; her brother James Paul McFadden for special photography, difficult to obtain; and to my husband, James L. McFadden, photographer, whose dedication to this work was untiring, and who supplied many of the black and white photographs which appear in the book.

To the staff of Douglas-West Publishers, my deepest appreciation for their enthusiasm for Oriental gardens in America, and the dedicated skills brought together in the production of this work.

Dorothy Loa McFadden
La Jolla, California

April 1976

Contents

A Note From the Author v
A Search for Serenity viii

PART I: ORIENTAL INFLUENCE ON GARDENS 1

Early Plant Hunters 3
Gardens of Old China 7
Traditional Gardens of Japan 21
Formal Gardens of India 37
Enchanted Gardens of Persia 41

PART II: A GUIDE TO ORIENTAL GARDENS IN AMERICA . 49

Invitation to America's Oriental Gardens 51
Annotated Bibliography 241
Alphabetical list of cities in which gardens are located 248

A Search for Serenity

Serenity lies at the base of all true Oriental gardens.

For many centuries the peoples of Asian countries have lived out their lives in villages and cities teeming with jostling humans and the discordant sounds of carts and animals—an endless medley of daily life. Only their gardens and temples provided respite. Here, for a while, one was removed from the world of haste and striving to a smaller world of tranquil contemplation. Surrounded by nature's quiet beauty or the gentle silence of holy ritual, one could look inward and take time to meditate upon the meaning of life, to restore inner peacefulness and find serenity of mind and spirit with which to continue life's journey.

Today, more than at any time in world history, people everywhere need the tranquility and ultimate serenity to be found in gardens. For many, there is a special kind of serenity in Oriental gardens once the restorative meanings behind the plantings and designs are understood. For here, quiet secluded places and gently winding paths are conducive to relaxed thought, and await all who need momentary solitude amid restful muted colors and remembered fragrances.

All gardens, great or small, hold these priceless gifts for beauty is, indeed, in the eye and mind of the beholder. Restoration of the human spirit surely must begin with serenity of mind and heart.

In the words of an ancient Oriental prophet who spoke with timeless wisdom:

Look upon rocks and flowers with inner sight—
and they will speak to you;

Listen with heart and mind to the sound of flowing water
and become one with brook and stream;

Lift up your face to the invisible magic of wandering winds
and the vast reaches of the Universe are yours to command.

. . . From The Book of Sayings of
Tsiang Samdup

Part One

Oriental Influence on Gardens

Early Plant Hunters

ALEXANDER SMITH (1830-1867)

Designing and planting gardens, tending and cherishing them, have been a part of life throughout the ages. Literature is filled with descriptions of gardens—all kinds of gardens from the exotic hanging gardens of Babylon to the little patch of flowers, tenderly cared for by early American settlers, which often was the only verdant spot of beauty in a vast prairieland.

The discovery and preservation of new varieties of plants, herbs, trees and shrubs for scientific purposes, and the pleasure derived from their beauty, have occupied mankind's interest for centuries. Early plant hunters were adventurers and intrepid explorers, frequently risking their lives in faraway places in search of botanical treasures. Getting to those distant areas where rare and medicinal plants flourished in natural wildness often meant facing challenging hazards. There were mountains to be crossed, rivers and seas to be navigated; and, most dreaded but most productive, dense jungles to be explored. The rivers usually were their routes of navigation, but the natives in many of these places were fearful of intruders and showed little friendliness.

During several centuries Chinese pirates roamed the rivers and

Detail of a woodblock print, about 1768, by Suzuki Harunobu (1725-1770)

seas in search of plunder or contraband, attacking commercial ships wherever encountered that were likely to be carrying valuable cargo. Smaller craft used by explorers in search of different kinds of treasure—botanical plants and herbs—often suffered the same fate. When no valuables were found, the pirates took vengeance. History records that many a valiant group of explorers during that period lost their lives and had their ships destroyed. Whatever specimens of plant life they had obtained also were lost.

The earliest plant hunters ventured forth alone, or in small parties, carrying only necessary supplies and equipment. But as the eighteenth century dawned, interest in botanical gardens and the medicinal qualities of many herbs and plants accelerated. Plant hunting gained the respect of both scientists and landscape designers. Expeditions, well equipped and financed, now ventured into all parts of the known world in search of herbs and plants for medicinal uses. Exotic trees and flowers for private and public gardens soon were in high favor with kings and potentates and their royal subjects. People, en masse, tended fields and vegetable gardens. Public gardens of exceptional beauty eventually emerged, often as gifts from some generous and wise ruler who understood the effects of beauty upon the lives of even the most humble.

Expeditions, under the guidance of horticultural societies and nurseries, now went forth for serious exploration. Most of these early expeditions originated in England and Russia; later from other European countries, and finally from America. Safety in hostile territories, most likely to provide the plant treasures sought by these expeditions, was not easily assured. Missionaries, however, served both God and Science through the discovery of rare plants and herbs with healing qualities on which frequently their lives depended. Flowers were cultivated out of a simple love for beauty.

Gardeners owe much to these special explorers. Many of the flowers, shrubs and trees found in America's gardens today were derived from cuttings and seed brought to the Western world from far lands. Some are still known by the names of their discoverers: *Rosa hugonis,* or Father Hugo's rose; Pissart's rose from Persia, with many lovely descendants. *Davidia involucrata,* the handkerchief tree, *Clematis Davidiana* and *Buddleia Davidii* are testimony to the discoveries and collections of Abbé David. Dozens of other plants, such as *Clematis montana Wilsonii,* resulted from years of dedicated searching and sacrifices by E. H. Wilson, familiarly known as "Chinese" Wilson to the botanical world after having made four trips into China. From only two of those journeys he brought back over 65,000 herbarium specimens; 1600 lots of seeds; and 168 clumps of plants and cuttings. Later, from a journey into Formosa (now Taiwan) during which headhunters became his guides under the protection of Japanese policemen, he obtained some of the rarest plants indigenous to that area.

American gardens, both public and private, flourish in beauty and color because of seeds, cuttings and plants also brought from the Orient.

The art of garden design, too, has been significantly influenced by Oriental ingenuity and sensitivity for many centuries throughout Europe and, more recently, North America; particularly in the United States, where interest in Oriental gardening has increased extensively since the early 1900s, focusing first upon gardens of Japan, and lately upon gardens of China, India and Persia.

Today, there are numerous private and public Oriental gardens in America. Over 100 of these are open to visitors' viewing, and provide extraordinary displays of beauty and color as well as quiet places for individual relaxation and meditation.

Information regarding public Oriental gardens in America, together with locations and directions for reaching them, is presented here for the first time in one collection.

Chinese garden embroidered on a silk screen. Courtesy of Mrs. Harley Cope. (James L. McFadden)

Gardens of Old China

A bridge flies away through a wild mist,
Yet here are the rocks and the fisherman's boat.
Oh, if only this river of floating peach-petals
Might lead me at last to the mythical cave!

THE PEACH-BLOSSOM RIVER
TRANSLATED BY WITTER BYNNER.
CHANG HSU, T'ANG DYNASTY

The innate artistry of the Chinese has been recognized for many centuries through their paintings, porcelains, bronzes and various other art forms. A study of Chinese garden designs will at once reveal a similarity in pattern to ancient hand scrolls; for here also picturesque scenes unroll gradually before the eyes of the viewer, never permitted to overwhelm by sudden bursts of myriad colors or confusing detail. This impression prevails not only in their public gardens but in those smaller courtyards of private dwellings where garden designs blend so unobtrusively that they seem to be watercolor sketches hanging upon each wall.

Underlying this pictorial artistry was the Taoist religion with emphasis upon solitary meditation by which man might achieve harmony with nature and his inner self. The early introduction of Buddhism into China merely intensified a desire to create a perpetual environment of natural beauty within which one could find peace and serenity. Gardens provided this perfect environment; for here were the very elements of universal rhythm—the natural flow of arrangement and untouched scenery which create a sense of restful order.

Traditional Chinese gardens, which featured rocks, mountains and water, date from the third century A.D. The palace gardens of the Emperor Yang Ti (605-618 A.D.) were perhaps the most extensive and elaborate. Built at the end of the sixth century, they encompassed an area of sixty square miles which was divided into sixteen segments. These included five lakes and seven small seas with islands. Each island was a sanctuary of peace with arbors and pavilions. A million men were required to handle the landscaping alone, for the hills and seas and lakes were artificially built. Ultimately, the emperor's extravagant absorption with expanding and maintaining his immense garden project brought about the downfall of the Sui Dynasty.

History repeated itself in the twelfth century A.D.

Emperor Hui Tsung (1101-1125 A.D.) was one of China's most respected artists. He was also an expert horticulturist. During his reign the Chinese passion for the use of grotesque rocks for garden ornaments reached its pinnacle. The emperor's special officer, Chu Mien, was ordered to collect such stones in the kingdom which might add to the beauty of the royal gardens. At that time and for many years, rocks of bizarre shapes and sizes were bought and sold for vast sums as if they were the rarest of precious jewels.

So engrossed was the emperor in building ever more splendid gardens that he ignored repeated warnings about the Mongol hordes whose armies were massing on his borders. Again, a great empire was lost for the sake of garden beauty. Hui Tsung died a captive of the Mongol ruler. Who is to say that he might not have regarded the beauty of his gardens well worth the price!

A century later, Marco Polo arrived at the court of the great Kublai Khan, where he found "a strange and mystical country of such extravagant beauty and wonders as to defy the senses." So impressed was he by the magnificence of the imperial deer parks, which encompassed hills and lakes and luxurious pavilions, that he remained at the emperor's court for many years recording for history the reality of the unbelievable world he had discovered. So accurate were Marco Polo's descriptions of Kublai Khan's man-made *Green Hill* that visitors today are able to identify it in modern Peking. The emperor had planted the area with a collection of unique trees. When a fine specimen was located, it was carefully extricated with the soil still protecting its roots, and transported by elephants to the imperial park. His purpose was not so much a desire to create an arboretum as to follow the advice of his astrologers. Those revered prophets had assured him that "whoever shall plant trees to beautify the earth, shall be rewarded by long life." One can only speculate upon the great Khan's interpretation of the prophesy. Perhaps the exotic natural beauty with which he surrounded himself was, indeed, the fulfillment of prophesy.

Toward the end of the eighteenth century an interlude of important changes in the creation of Chinese gardens developed. Emperor Ch'ien Lung (1736-1795 A.D.) summoned Father Benôit, a French Jesuit missionary, and requested that a garden in the French style of Le Nôtre be created at the royal summer palace outside Peking. Father Benôit responded with extraordinary skills and artistry. To the amazement of the emperor and his subjects, the *Garden of Gardens* emerged with elaborate cascades operated by hydraulic machinery. While this garden lacked the precise geometrical designs which characterized Le Nôtre's gardens, it introduced into gardening art an amusing combination of gay Baroque and traditional Chinese.

Unfortunately none of those early royal gardens survived. By tradition, no palace, including its surrounding garden, could be used as a dwelling by any succeeding emperor. Such buildings were simply abandoned and left to decay; and since they were made of wood, even the ruins soon vanished. Except for records made by individuals such as Marco Polo or an occasional abbot or priest during these periods, the very existence of those luxurious gardens might have been lost altogether. But we know that during Marco Polo's time not only emperors and their high officials maintained vast landscape gardens, but wealthy citizens and scholars as well. We also know that peasants, whose small tracts of land scarcely provided enough food for their families, bitterly resented such "waste of good land." Many centuries would pass before this waste would be remedied. Perhaps the souls of those ancient tillers of the soil may now rest in peace; for the Imperial Gardens in the People's Republic of China today belong to the people as public parks where all workers may find rest and recreation.

As previously noted, the great landscape gardens of China covered vast areas which encompassed significant features essential to such gardens—rocks, hills, small mountains, and always water; for these elements are symbols of spiritual importance under Oriental teachings. So important were such elements that, if not naturally present, they were artificially created to provide the desired artistic design and, in the process, simultaneously create great hollows in the earth which ultimately became the basins for lakes and streams.

In a similar manner, favorite scenes which existed many miles away often were reproduced artificially. Artistic winding paths, each turn carefully planned to surprise the stroller with some exquisite view, provided passage through the extensive areas devoted to landscaped garden parks; for there were no roads in these areas. Decorative bridges spanned small lakes and streams, always carefully placed so that their reflections might add beauty to the scene.

Garden pavilions also were placed in especially lovely spots beside lakes or natural streams which reflected their beauty. Small pavilions with gracefully upturned roofs painted in bright colors offered shelter or privacy, or moments of comfort while enjoying a particularly spellbinding scene such as flowering trees in springtime or the glory of autumn's colors. Capturing the mystic qualities of a landscape by moonlight, or when snow mantled hills and mountains and lakes, were moments to treasure for a lifetime.

The large pavilions were designed for entertaining friends with wine-drinking and song. For evening parties, the gardens were decorated with gauze lanterns of many colors and illuminated by flowered lanterns. Some of the smaller pavilions, however, served a dual purpose. Poets, musicians and artists often used them while composing poems and songs, or recording the image of a lovely scene. For these creators of beauty, a thoughtful host sometimes provided a special interior wall where a picture might be painted or a song poem inscribed at high moments of inspiration.

Surely Li Tai-pe must have found such a pavilion—a quiet place of isolation—in which to compose that magnificent poem, *The Porcelain Pavilion:*

> *In the middle of the lake we made*
> *Is a porcelain house all green and white.*

> *Thither we walk on a bridge of jade,*
> *Arched like the back of a tiger.*
> *In this pavilion sit our friends*
> *In garments light, and drink their wine*
> *With merry talk, or writing verse.*
> *Their heavy headgear they discard*
> *And turn their sleeves a little up . . .*

A favorite game among these happy gentlemen, while strolling beside a stream, was to float an empty wine cup on the water, then command each passerby to compose a poem instantly or pay a penalty by drinking a large draught of wine. Frequently, to induce the Muse, poets might spend many hours or even entire days gliding over a quiet lake in an elaborately decorated and luxuriously furnished "dragon boat."

Whether of natural or artificial construction, lakes and islands in landscape gardens are essential to Chinese design and always are irregular in shape. The size might vary, but irregularity in design was thought to better portray the natural islands and lakes which have certain spiritual significance. There is a Chinese legend about three magic isles floating upon an Eastern ocean, where wise beings who had learned the secrets of immortality dwelt in peaceful contemplation forever. This legend may be the basis for the Chinese association of islands with longevity and happiness. Later Buddhist monks originated the solitary symbolic island concept from which a central peak towered majestically above cloud mists, its base surrounded by enduring rocks. The whole represented the universe.

Rocks have always played a significant part in Chinese gardens. Usually these were of strange, even grotesque, shapes. The use of such rocks began with the earliest known imperial gardens. No royal garden was without many such formations, standing tall, with varied symbolic meanings—some with animal-like faces. Quantities of such rocks were found in Lake Tai-hu, near Soochow. Apparently the currents of the lake are very strong there, for the limestone, taken from the bottom of the lake, is completely perforated with deep holes that give it the appearance of an enormous porous sponge.

Color predominated in almost every object to be found in landscaped gardens of China from earliest times—brightly enameled pavilions and pagodas, glazed or painted bridges, a rosebush or flowering plumtree planted beside a shelter's window or carefully placed throughout a garden to accent other colors. Sometimes there were sweeping stretches of wild flowers, the variety of colors dependent upon the seasons for natural blooming. Ponds and lakes were patterned with lotus blossoms and water lilies of varied hues. But always the desired effect was subtle and restrained, never garish or startling.

The uses of color by Chinese landscape garden designers often were combined with a sense of drama. A quiet, happy section of the garden also presented a contrasting terror such as overhanging rocks, strangely deformed trees, a mysterious dark cave, or the thunder of a roaring waterfall. Intermittently, other caves scattered about such parklands were designed as cool retreats from the summer heat. It was during this relatively brief period, around 1000 A.D., that interest in paintings of individual blossoms focused attention upon a wider use of brightly colored flowers in Chinese gardens. This trend did not last very long. The old simplicity, which had endured for thousands of years, returned. The objective was to recreate nature rather than obscure it by great masses of color.

While most historical records of Chinese gardens seem to have concentrated upon imperial or other extensive gardens, there were, of course, many smaller gardens adjoining the homes of city dwellers. A man of wealth might surround his gardens with several walls: an exterior wall for protection; an inner wall for privacy with narrow alleys to provide passage for visitors without revealing prematurely the beauty that awaited them; and, finally, the walls of the house itself with its surrounding courtyards. Here, outside areas were planned for living comfort as were the interior rooms of the house. Vistas were carefully designed and created so that one could see into the house with varied perspective, but always as if viewing a small scene in a beautiful frame. Perhaps one found a unique circular or hexagonal Chinese "moon gate"; or a particularly lovely plant arrangement inside, seen through glazed fretwork windows or an opening resembling a vase; a stylized flower bud, or a delicate unfurled Chinese fan.

The walls of the courtyards also were brightened by these uniquely designed window frames, or ceramic medallions placed at various heights. The garden plantings themselves were few but carefully chosen: a bed of white chrysanthemums or peonies, a flowering tree, a small grove of bamboo, a low palmetto, grasses and a few foliage plants. In the center place of honor, there was often a treasured pitted rock; or if the home was that of a wealthy owner there might be an entire wall of grotesque and strangely shaped rocks. At intervals about the garden stood carved stone benches or barrel-shaped stools which invited family or guests to stay a while for a cup of tea, and take time to admire the garden.

The plans for some of these home garden complexes were most elaborate.

The Liu Garden in Soochow, built in the sixteenth century, is a fascinating example. There were two courts which could be enjoyed from the garden room by means of folding doors on two sides. The central pavilion was bordered by a pool terrace, which also had a garden room and more small courtyards arranged at each end, one of which was framed by wisteria vines. One entire side of that area was enclosed by a white "dragon wall" with tiles arranged in an undulating design extending along the top of the wall.

At the back of the pavilion was a second garden room and courtyard. On the opposite side, a series of three libraries, a theater, and at one far secluded corner, a study. The entire spacious structure was a carefully planned home which provided gracious living and hospitality, with the necessary quiet and solitude for meditation or scholarly pursuits.

Flowers in Chinese gardens at that period never were used in colorful profusion as in gardens of most other countries, especially English gardens. Rarely, if ever, were they used strictly as color accents in a garden plan. Fragrance, form and symbolic significance, even in flower arrangements for the home, were of first importance. In old China, every blossom used in landscape gardening or potted courtyard plantings had special meaning and was selected for that reason.

Through the teachings of Buddhism the lotus, symbolizing purity, was highly revered. It grew or was planted almost everywhere—on ponds and lakes, in garden pools and in large containers which would be moved from place to place. As with water lilies, the lotus also sprang from lowly mud, but achieved great beauty.

This symbolism has been passed down to modern times in terms of aspiration and inspiration.

The peony signifies, variously, aristocracy or wealth. The peach tree, longevity; while peach blossoms symbolically refer either to a beautiful woman, or fragility in terms of success or lifespan. The pine tree also signifies longevity but more in terms of steadfastness or ruggedness. The bamboo stands for modesty and flexibility. These, together with the plum tree, signify the highest virtues of Chinese culture.

Of all these, the plum tree is perhaps the most beloved.

During the Sung dynasty, legend records, an emperor composed over a thousand poems to this simple flower. Even today the plum tree is recommended in a Chinese paperback guide book, giving twenty-six different uses or ways to display its beauty. Among these: combining plum with willows so that the foliage of each provides contrasts even after the plum blossoms have fallen; use as a frontispiece with pine and bamboo to accentuate the plum's coloring; on a stream's embankment, or beside a small bridge or narrow fence; or arranged to provide a vista from a favorite window. In legend and song, plum, pine and bamboo were considered "winter friends" meaning the opposite of a modern expression, "fair-weather friends."

Chinese poets for many centuries have written poetic descriptions of the beauty found in simple things. None has been so revered by poets as the opening of a flower bud. A modern writer tells of an old Chinese gentleman who stood for hours silently bending over an unfurling peony blossom. In ancient times, when a budding plant was brought into the family courtyard, placed in an ornamental pot, and set in a carefully selected position, it was watched with devout attention during its full life cycle; through maturing, blossom time, and on to gradual withering and final death. This flower-cycle in happy contemplation represented the life cycle of man: growth, perfection and decline.

Flowers of all kinds, however, did appear in Chinese gardens although, as emphasized earlier, always in a restrained, modest manner; never in flamboyant masses of color.

Most prevalent in old Chinese gardens were camellias, roses, lilies and poppies, along with a few other flowers carefully selected for fragrance rather than color. Wisteria had long been a favorite for decorating walls or for framing a view. White was a favorite color, used to accent delicate colors, except with chrysanthemums where yellow always reigned supreme.

Flowering trees—apricot, pomegranate, loquat, cherry, peach, plum—all were valued more for their blossoms than for their fruits. Through the astute study of Chinese paintings, modern horticulturists have been able to compile long lists of the kinds of flowers grown by the Chinese through many centuries.

In Oriental countries flowers have always been an integral part of life, whether one single blossom in a poor man's courtyard, or flowers in abundance to satisfy an emperor's whim. One such emperor commanded that his bed be placed next to a blossoming tree so that he would not miss a moment of the flowers' life cycle. Another demanded that the stairs to his royal gardens be strewn with lotus flowers so that the feet of his beloved would never touch the barren stones.

The Chinese people always have bestowed pretty names upon even the lowliest flowers, many of which are equally charming in translations. Among the chrysanthemums the small yellow button-size blossom is called "Heaven Full of Stars"; the white quill-type flower is "Goose-Feathers Tube"; the yellow quill, "Carrot Threads"; the large ragged violet one, "Drunk-with-Wine-made-from-Peaches-of-the-Immortals." For every flower, and all its relatives, the names bestowed are meaningful and selected with affection and respect.

CHINESE INFLUENCE ON EUROPEAN GARDENS

In the late eighteenth century, "Capability" Brown, Humphrey Repton, and other English landscape architects introduced revolutionary ideas for "natural" gardens as against formal flowerbeds. The movement created much controversy which was further stimulated by reports coming out of China about magnificent landscape gardens which seemed to challenge England's reputation as the country of gardeners and designers.

Descriptions of Chinese gardens provided by French missionary Father Attiret, and by Père J. B. Du Halde's book on the Chinese Empire, became topics of the day at literary salons and aristocratic

social gatherings. English gardens had expanded to a limited degree experimentally into the creation of gardens which reproduced natural landscapes. Nothing as extensive or lavish as the Chinese gardens described by the French missionaries had been undertaken. But as discussions among gardening circles, horticulturists, and newspaper articles intensified, the colorful descriptions of ornamental structures, such as garden and lakeside or island pavilions, soon captured the imagination of European architects. Sir William Chambers had spent some time in China while in the service of the Swedish East India Company and had studied architecture in Italy, becoming architectural tutor to the Prince of Wales (later King George III). His authority during that period was unquestioned, and was further strengthened by his first book, *Designs for Chinese Buildings,* published in 1757. Moreover, Augusta, mother of George II, commissioned Sir William to prepare designs and landscaping for gardens which would surround the royal residence—the Kew Gardens of today. Although a number of Chinese structures were built, only the Pagoda is still standing in these famous gardens.

With the construction of Kew Gardens, however, the Chinese influence on English gardens quickly spread. Dainty pavilions, bridges, aviaries and pagodas began to appear in the "landscape gardens" of private estates throughout England. The "craze" for *chinoiseries* soon spread to wallpaper designs, furniture, tiling and frescoes.

During the next decades enthusiasm for Chinese architecture and decorations became increasingly evident in other European countries: Austria, Belgium, France, Germany, Holland, Italy, Russia, Spain and Sweden.

At Wilhelmshoehe, near Cassel, Germany, a "Chinese Village" was built which included a farm with barns, stables, a dairy, a pagoda, and houses for the village attendants. It was unfortunate that no Chinese farm laborers could be found in Germany at that time; African women tended the gardens.

Catherine II of Russia ordered her English landscape architect to design a "Chinese Village" at Tsarskoie, near Leningrad. The village consisted of eighteen small houses, a miniature temple and a pagoda. Its English garden contained Chinese bridges, some with decorative Oriental figures.

Detail from an etching and aquatint entitled "A Concert at Vauxhill Gardens" by Thomas Rowlandson. (Courtesy Metropolitan Museum of Art)

Some of these Chinese-inspired structures still exist in England and on the continent. Most were more fanciful than authentic, and few if any of the actual gardens followed the principles underlying Chinese garden philosophy.

This growing interest in Chinese cultural arts, however, was not confined exclusively to gardens and architecture. Writers, historical and fictional, and philosophers began to contribute extensively to knowledge of China's arts and customs and religious beliefs. Merchants and other travelers throughout the Far East brought back *objets d'art* and first-hand reports on customs, books, and of the people themselves.

The age of modern intercultural exchange had dawned.

NOTES FOR TRAVELERS TO CHINA

It is still difficult to obtain permission to visit China as a casual sightseer, but if one *is* granted such permission, no up-to-date guidebooks are available. Information, therefore, must be confined to generalities.

The palace gardens in Peking have been preserved, parts of them now used by the workers for recreation and rest periods. *Fodor's Guide; Peking,* written in 1972, provides considerable information about these gardens. There are superb photographic illustrations in Burland's *Travels of Marco Polo,* showing the Green Hill on an island in Peking which the great explorer describes, as well as summer houses and gardens in Soochow, and a temple courtyard garden in Canton. Wheeler's *Splendors of the East* also has recent pictures of gardens; and Loraine E. Kuck's *The Art of the Japanese Garden* has a complete chapter on gardens in China, as of 1940, which would be worth studying before making the journey (see bibliography).

Travelers to Taiwan are likely to find much Western influence in gardens and plantings. However, there are a number of public parks and areas where Chinese decorative features prevail—pagodas, pavilions, and man-made lakes with lotus flowers floating in the placid waters. There is a long serpentine bridge on Cheng Ching Lake at Kaohsiung in southern Taiwan, which is very unusual and worth the journey for a sightseer. Its unique design had purpose as well as artistry—the nine turns it makes in crossing the lake is believed to evade evil spirits which can only move in a straight line.

Yangming Park at Taipei is delightfully colorful, especially when cherry trees and wisteria are in bloom. Taipei Park and Shuang Hsi Park, located in a Taipei suburb, have Chinese architectural detail such as artificial hills, strange rocks, and pine and bamboo plantings.

Traditional Gardens of Japan

In the city fields
  contemplating
  cherry trees . . .
Strangers are like friends.

ISSA

Many excellent books on the underlying philosophy and art of Japanese gardens are now available in most public libraries. Such works have greatly stimulated American interest in the garden art of this Oriental country. Comprehension of their religious and somewhat mystical approach to the creation of their gardens, however, has not been so quickly attained by Westerners. Some knowledge of the basic history of Japanese gardens, as they evolved through several centuries, is certain to create a better understanding of that art and to provide more complete enjoyment of Japanese gardens in America and other parts of the world.

Japan is a country endowed with great natural beauty. It is not surprising, therefore, that its gardens should take forms and designs closely identified with nature—the natural wonders of mountains, streams, waterfalls and growing things. Children are taught from earliest childhood to show reverence for these wonders. Many of these, such as bamboo, pine trees, and certain mountains, are regarded as holy, to be approached ceremonially with burning incense and prayers.

The sea always has provided the Japanese people with essential

Tôfukuji Temple, Kyoto, Japan. View of the garden from the Founder's Hall. (Japan National Tourist Organization)

foods; thus, water has a special place in their religious rituals. During their early history these Japanese islands were isolated from the rest of the known world. Not until the seventh century A.D. was there travel and commerce even with neighboring Korea. Later, when commerce had expanded into mainland China, travelers from Japan to the vast Chinese empire beheld for the first time stupendous parks—some as large as sixty miles in circumference—created for the Emperor Yang Ti. These were artificially landscaped areas with hills, lakes and islands, dotted with colorful bridges and pavilions. Soon after the Japanese Ambassador Ono ro Imoko returned from China in 607 A.D., the first history of Japanese gardening was recorded.

The early Japanese landscaped gardens were fairly authentic adaptations of those gardens found in China. That is, they displayed the same art forms: mountains built of assembled rocks, lakes and many islands, cascades, and the ever-present scarlet bridges.

Such gardens, for many years, were created only to surround the imperial palace; but as the site of government frequently changed from one location to another, landscaped gardens of great beauty began to appear in various parts of Japan. One of the most beautiful, and still a mecca for garden lovers, was in Kyoto (then called Heian-kyo), "the capital of Peace and Tranquility." Here the pleasure gardens which surrounded the imperial buildings covered more than thirty-three acres. These were used as settings for elaborate entertainments, poetry contests and feasts similar to the earlier garden parties of China's emperors or, in later years, those given by Italy's most noble families.

One of the most authentic descriptions of Japanese gardens and the way of life during that period may be found in a delightful novel, *The Tale of Genji,* written by an aristocratic lady of the Heian period (about 1000 A.D.). She tells of the "many apartments for his ladies" in Prince Genji's house, each with its own lovely private garden which he himself had planned. Her descriptions of those gardens, each individual in design and plant arrangements, may well have served designers in much later periods. A book on garden art, which was written for a wealthy gentleman some years after the novel, gives detailed instructions for placing stones and plants precisely and for designing lakes and ponds which are compatible with nature. It must be assumed that the gentleman for whom the book was written was personally involved with the gardens' creation, giving proper instructions to his workmen!

As Zen Buddhism began to spread into Japan, the influence of that philosophy on gardening soon became apparent. For the first time, rules were set down for placing rocks which conformed precisely with the symbolism represented.

Tea was introduced into Japan by Zen Buddhists in the twelfth century A.D. The tea cult, however, and the building of houses with gardens surrounding them, did not develop until the fourteenth and fifteenth centuries. The beautiful moss gardens which have long been greatly admired were created during that period, in addition to the dry sand-and-stone gardens which were most frequently used around temples. Inevitably, the Zen mysticism which creates an indefinable atmosphere in any Japanese garden began to emerge, and still remains at the present time.

Except for an occasional red lacquer bridge, the colorful accents of the Chinese gardens were gradually set aside. Authentic Japanese gardens were designed as monochromes in subdued shades of green and gray. Garden structures, such as temples and homes, were usually built of natural dark wood.

During the nineteenth century many fine parks of great size were laid out for public uses. Elaborate, spacious gardens were created around the homes of the wealthy. But as population increased, limiting the space available for public or private gardens on these islands, designing underwent many changes. The objective of the designer now became one of reproducing features of Japan's beloved landscape in smaller areas. Home gardens were so designed that the families could admire them from indoors by pushing the paper-screen wall (*shojis*) aside. Seated on the floor, they could contemplate a small replica of some distant mountain, lake, or waterfall and rock formations. Many of these were authentic duplicates in miniature of a favorite scene.

The relationship between the new Japanese gardens and China's vast landscaped gardens which had originally inspired their creation was no longer so apparent. The Japanese people had developed a quite distinctive garden art form of their own. With this new art form an elusive quality of understatement is evident in all Japanese gardens on the islands today, and in replicas in other countries as well as in America.

The underlying philosophy of Japanese garden designs is one of subtle balance—the *Yin* and *Yang* of components. These symbolize male and female, the strong and the weak, in harmonious contrast. Often there is one unfinished element, a subtle stimulation of the viewer's imagination. Above all, the total effect of such gardens must be nature-inspired and always subtly achieved by the creative process of the designer; *his* concept of what his eyes behold. Western visitors to Japanese gardens should not try to penetrate their mysteries but, instead, merely accept their gifts of beauty and absorb the serenity of mind and spirit offered.

Elements of Design

Authentic, traditionally designed Japanese gardens fall into three general classifications: hill-and-water gardens; flat or dry gardens; and tea gardens.

Hill-and-water gardens may be large or small, secluded behind a house, or covering great public spaces. Each, however, is carefully planned to achieve a look of naturalness—a landscape untouched by man. Some may be viewed only from inside the house, while others are "stroll gardens" with winding paths which beckon the stroller to follow and may, at times, incorporate a flat garden in some suitable place.

Flat or dry gardens are usually composed entirely of sand or gravel raked into patterns which suggest waves, using rocks to represent islands; some are chosen for religious symbolism. However, they may be fashioned with stones and pebbles which are arranged to simulate a stream-bed. Imagination fills the stream with placid water! A rock, or group of stones, placed vertically represents a waterfall, again requiring the imagination of the beholder to supply the water. This kind of subtlety contributes both eye appeal and spiritual stimulation; for the flat-dry gardens are closely aligned with Zen philosophy. Devotees may sit silently for hours contemplating the many spiritual symbolisms. Some flat gardens use real streams, gushing from miniature waterfalls. Another beautiful form is the moss garden consisting entirely of lovely green velvet patches under slender deciduous trees through which the sun's rays slant, making dappled patterns of light and shadow.

The tea garden is the most formal. It is designed according to strictest rules, for it is here that Zen Buddhists gather in the teahouse to observe ceremony. Usually there is a small, rather simple outer garden from which a winding path of stepping stones leads to a meticulously planned middle garden, composed of replicas of deep woods or mountain scenes. The path also serves to prepare the visitors' minds for the tranquility and religious meditation which await them. At the teahouse, visitors wash their hands and rinse their mouths with the water that flows through a bamboo spout into a stone purification basin. This ritual cleanses them of the sins and cares of the world. A tall simple stone lantern stands near the basin, its light supplied by a candle placed inside it just before evening ceremonies.

The entrance to the teahouse is small and very low, requiring those who enter to bend so low as to almost creep inside. The ceremony is usually observed in two ritualistic sessions, with a bench provided for visitors to rest upon during the interval.

Water is a constantly recurring element in Japanese gardens. Even the smallest gardens have some water element in their design. This is not surprising since Japan is composed of hundreds of islands, and its people always have lived close to the sea; frequent rainfall produces torrential waterfalls and rivers.

Large Japanese gardens included huge ponds and often lakes. The borders of these lakes when artificially constructed were always of irregular design, conforming to the contours of natural lakes, with occasional rocks carefully placed with plants and mosses concealing the new raw edges. (This principle unfortunately is often ignored in Japanese gardens in America, with masses of cement exposed which destroys the desired illusion of naturalness.) The shape of a lake's design varied, but most frequently used was that of the crane, or the Chinese character for "heart." During the rule of the shoguns, lakes in landscaped gardens were so extensive they could accommodate elaborate boats for entertainment and social affairs.

Ornamental features, such as pagodas or lanterns, are carefully placed at shorelines to duplicate beauty from reflections in the water. Pine trees, near the water's edge, are trained to bend as they grow into forms that create striking silhouettes. Stones are arranged in decorative designs at intervals in selected spots or groups at the water's edge.

The Japanese revere the carp, or *koi,* out of respect for its ability to swim upstream and leap a waterfall. Every lake sparkles with the brilliant gold, red and black of these remarkable creatures.

Islands also are of great importance in Japanese gardens, even as they were in China. Their shape and location always have religious significance. A popular design is the "turtle island," made from grouping gray-brown stones into the shape of the sacred turtle. A series of little grass mounds, close together, may support a miniature shrine dedicated to the spirit of the lake, assuring the owner good fortune.

Bridges are, of course, almost synonymous with Oriental gardens and landscaped parks. Japanese bridges, with high arches and of brilliant red color, are direct derivations of early Chinese designs. The origin of this design had significance; for added beauty was derived from the semi-circular contour which, with reflection in the water below, completed the design that is popularly named "moon bridge."

"Drum bridges" are made of dark natural wood; they are a solemn contrast to the dramatic flashes of the red bridges. Picturesque bridges for crossing small streams are constructed from reeds and bamboo with sodded paths connecting with the natural paths which lie at both ends of the bridge. Bridges made from planks often are zigzagged instead of crossing in a straight line; for it was believed that this diverted evil spirits who were able to move only in a straight line! A more practical, and perhaps spiritual, interpretation was that by slowing the pace of the traveler he had time for quiet meditation during the crossing.

Garden Components

Rocks. An important element in Japanese garden design is the use of rocks. The shapes and sizes vary, but the relationship of each shape and size to other rocks may have special meanings sometimes difficult for Westerners to understand. For example, in Kyoto's famous Zen garden of Daisen-in there are thirty different stones with significant names such as *turtle-head, splash-of-waves, tiger's head, water-imp, white cloud, Buddha's foot impression,* and other equally fanciful names. Larger gardens may have more than one hundred forty stones with individual names. These rocks are grouped in five general classifications: tall vertical, low vertical, arching, horizontal, and reclining. Each grouping has a subtle symbolism and must be placed according to fixed rules. Balance must be maintained between male and female stones in all arrangements.

Throughout Japan, "rock nurseries" are prevalent. Here one may buy just the right stones to express the desired symbolisms or artistic effects. Selecting the stones is never done casually; only after hours or days of serious thought and discussion. (Need one emphasize that no Japanese garden designer would stoop to using imitation rock made of cement!)

Large rocks are also used for special purposes. These may represent mountains which create background for diversified landscapes, or to form grottos and caves. Frequently such rocks are placed beside a pathway to provide a resting place for visitors.

Paths. Pathways are important in any garden. The surface of a path may be of earth or constructed of flat stones carefully chosen and arranged, but its design is always irregular, twisting and turning to provide surprise views and vistas. Occasionally the path may seem to disappear altogether. To an imaginative viewer this implies a sense of great distance.

Gates, walls, fences. The beautifully designed *torii* gateway is a familiar feature in almost every Japanese garden to be found outside Japan itself. It is regrettable that garden designers seem unaware that the *torii* gate has religious significance in Japan and is used only as the entrance to a Shinto place of worship. They should never be used as mere ornamental garden fixtures, or used at the entrance to announce the name of the garden.

Garden gates are always constructed from dark natural wood, with a small roof shelter and doors decorated by geometric designs, and set into a whitewashed wall or bamboo fence which conceals the garden from public view. Other walls or fences which surround the planted areas may be of wood, stone, bamboo or hedges. Short fences of ornamental woven reeds or bamboo are frequently used for partitions in some areas of the garden to provide seclusion or solitude for quiet meditation. Or these also may be used to conceal an undesirable outlook! But if there is a fine view beyond the garden, or a graceful tree in a neighbor's yard, the fence is kept low for mutual enjoyment of "borrowed scenery."

Lanterns. To many Westerners, the stone lantern has become merely a trademark to identify a Japanese garden. In Japan, however, lanterns, as with the *torii,* have much more significance. Garden lanterns are chosen with great care, and much attention is given to the size of the lantern for a particular use.

Stone lanterns are placed beside pathways, or near the water basin at teahouses. They are used extensively at Shinto shrines and temples, both for lighting and expressions of reverence. At the Shinto Kasuga shrine of Nara, some three thousand stone lanterns line its approach, each lantern an "offering" from a different worshipper. These stone lanterns receive special attention, often rubbed with dry earth which is believed to encourage growth of the mosses and lichens, and add the beauty of age. One lantern of special design is called "snow-viewing lantern." Its broad top is shaped to capture a decorative mound of snow. Bronze pedestal lanterns of much larger sizes are used in public places for lighting effects.

Ornamentals. Stone pagodas, although of religious origin, often are used to create tall accents where balance of composition is required. These vary in height from three to thirteen stories—but never an even number! Such pagodas add beauty when placed near pools or lakes to provide reflections. Very large gardens sometimes use tall, brightly painted wooden pagodas as especially striking ornamental features.

Statues of various "gods" or symbolic creatures are also popular as ornamental objects. The turtle and the crane symbolize happiness and longevity.

Plants and flowers. The trees and shrubs used in Japanese gardens are almost entirely evergreens which achieve year-round beauty. As with stones and lanterns, these also are chosen to create form and texture contrasts; and evergreens are spectacular when mantled with new-fallen snow.

Variety of color, as mentioned earlier, is never the objective with Japanese garden designers who tend to emphasize monochrome effects. Imagine the subtle impression of a garden landscape composed entirely of shrubs and trees of varied shades of green. Only occasionally will the designer permit the fall coloring of Japanese maple trees to break this monotone scheme with gently falling leaves.

Trees and shrubs in Japanese gardens require considerable care, and must be regularly clipped and pruned to retain size and shape. The art of shaping plants and trees into geometric designs has been handed down from father to son in Japan, and consists of many exacting rules. "Cloud-pruning," for instance, is more readily achieved with some trees or shrubs than others. It is the precise art of accenting each branch and keeping it separated from all others so that growth is in layers, assuming the form of a dense cloud or cushion. (Such shaping may be seen throughout California, fortunate in having many Japanese gardeners.) Training branches into the desired position or direction for artistic effects, or the protection of the branches themselves from the weight of heavy snowfall, is also a special art. Poles and frameworks of bamboo are used, and must be precisely placed. To Western visitors, these "crutches" may seem unsightly, but not to the Japanese who see only the desired design!

Flowerbeds, per se, which are essential to almost every American and English garden, are totally absent from Japanese gardens. An occasional clump of iris or a blossoming cherry or plum tree provide the only color notes. Water lilies decorate lakes and ponds and are admired both for their beauty and their religious meanings. But no expert Japanese garden designer ever would introduce mounds of garish magenta azaleas which, alas, are so often seen in Japanese American gardens. Colors that virtually shriek aloud disturb the placidity which is a vital part of any genuine Japanese garden scene.

There are, of course, rare exceptions. At the Meiji Shrine gardens in Tokyo, displays of blossoming iris may be seen, but their colors are muted, blending softly with their surroundings. They attract thousands of Japanese visitors and travelers from other countries. Chrysanthemums, traditionally linked with Japanese horticulture, are never planted in "garden plots." Instead, they are grown in urns or flowerpots strictly for indoor flower arrangements, and to compete in chrysanthemum shows which are held annually in many cities of Japan. In recent years, however, since the influx of Western materials and manners, a growing interest in the cultivation of "garden flowers" has come about. Whether this is to be a temporary "fad" or an enduring trend, only time can tell.

JAPANESE INFLUENCE ON GARDENS OF EUROPE

In his splendid book *The Story of Gardening*, which is now a classic, Richardson Wright comments: "The Japanese garden is a type of imitative landscaping that does not stand travel." His use of the phrase "imitative landscaping" suggests that he did not understand the true philosophy of these gardens, and was convinced that they would never be adopted in other countries!

England has never shown much interest in Japanese garden art since, for the English, gardens mean flowers. However, there are a few famous Japanese gardens at Fanham Hall in Ware-Herts (now owned by The Westminster Bank), which cover five acres, with a Japanese house imported from the International Exhibition in Paris, which, of course, was originally designed by a Japanese.

There is also a smaller Japanese water garden at Charleton, Kilconquhar, Fifeshire, Scotland. On a famous breeding farm for blooded horses near Kildare, thirty miles southwest of Dublin, Ireland, travelers will find an exquisite Japanese stroll garden that was created for Lord Wavertree by his Japanese gardener, Eida, and his son, Minoruje, which symbolizes through stages in the design the experiences a man may encounter from birth to death.

There are only a few well-known examples of Japanese gardens on the continent of Europe. At the UNESCO Building in Paris, sculptor Isamo Noguchi designed an authentic flat stone-and-gravel meditation garden, *The Japanese Garden of Peace.* In Clingendael Park at the Hague, Holland, there is an exceptionally beautiful Japanese moss garden. (It can be visited only in May, with a permit obtained by the visitor's hotel porter from the Parks Department.) At Dortmund, Germany, the Westfalenpark has a lovely hillside garden of Japanese design, complete with an authentic teahouse brought from Japan. Undoubtedly there are others in Europe if one has the time and the inclination to search for them.

JAPANESE GARDENS IN AMERICA

The Japanese exhibit at the Philadelphia Centennial Exposition of 1876 is credited with having introduced both the Japanese style house and their gardens to the American public. The reaction, at first, was not overwhelmingly favorable. It was all so odd and different! Gradually, however, visitors ventured a closer look and became intrigued by the uniqueness and quiet loveliness of these gardens; the simplicity and sense of openness found in their house designs. It was unfortunate, however, that this particular garden was not authentic Japanese. A description of it, written at that time, reads: "The flower beds are laid out neatly and fenced in with bamboo. Screens of matting and dried grass divide the parterres. There is a fountain, guiltless of a jet-d' eau, from which the water trickles. A queer shaped urn of granite on a pedestal [probably a stone lantern—ed.] shows marks of great age, weatherworn and dilapidated. The garden statuary is peculiar. Bronze figures of storks, six to eight feet high, stand in groups at certain places, and a few bronze pigs are disposed in easy comfort in shady places."

Many later expositions included better Japanese exhibits. The Southern Exposition at Louisville, Kentucky, in 1883, displayed a "Japanese Village." The World's Columbian Exposition in San Francisco in 1894 used Japanese sections; and at California's Midwinter Exposition in 1903 there were extensive Japanese displays including an imperial garden. Frequently the buildings from such lavish expositions were later moved to permanent sites in various parts of the United States. This continued exposure to garden viewers and designers of a new and different art soon began to have its influence on American gardens. A trend developed. It was considered fashionable for lavish estates of the wealthy to include a Japanese garden when planning the landscaping for these spacious grounds. Unfortunately, only a few of these have survived. (Seven of these gardens are included in this volume; they are now open for public viewing.)

In the early part of the twentieth century Japan introduced a new attraction to American public gardens and parks: the exquisite Japanese cherry tree. The first of these came as a gift to the American government from the city of Tokyo—600 saplings and grafts from the Arawaka Canal area of Japan. About 550 of these were of the Yoshin variety; 50 were Akebono. During more than three-quarters of a century, these magnificent trees have multiplied and other varieties have been added. Some were gifts from Oriental friends of America; others, gifts from individual Americans in tribute to a profound admiration for Oriental gardens. President Taft's wife planted the first cherry trees along the banks of the Potomac. Today thousands of people make a yearly pilgrimage to Washington, D.C., for the National Cherry Blossom Festival, usually in April when the trees are in full bloom. The trees extend along a six-mile promenade, representing one of the most lavish displays of beauty to be found anywhere in the world. Color, fragrance, and a profound feeling of awe virtually overwhelm one's senses. In recent years as the number of visitors increased, more reserved seats were provided for enjoying the annual parades with bands and spectacular floats.

Another superb display of Japanese cherry trees is in Branch Brook Park at Newark, New Jersey, which began with a gift of 2050 cherry trees imported from Japan by Mrs. Felix Fuld in 1927. Here, too, cherry blossom time is usually the last week in April and the first week of May. During these weeks thousands of visitors drive slowly through the park, many repeating the drive several times. This is one of the most comprehensive plantings of cherry trees in the United States.

Few visitors would want to miss the lovely display of cherry blossoms to be seen in Brooklyn Botanic Gardens in New York. This garden also began as a gift from Japan. Since its inauguration, many more trees were added, and the garden now displays some twenty to thirty different varieties of Japanese cherry trees.

These and other plantings of Japanese cherry trees throughout America are annual reminders of these gifts of friendship—a kind of rare beauty which Japan always has so eagerly shared with us. Many American gardeners now include one or two of these lovely trees in their own private gardens and enjoy each stage of their beauty—pearly blossoms at sunrise, at sunset, and sometimes at night (as shown by the charming Japanese lady in the illustration who is holding up a lantern to enjoy the flowers' beauty against the night sky).

The steadily growing interest in gardens and more authentic garden designs brought about an ever-widening enthusiasm for

---

Japanese cherry trees in bloom, opposite the Jefferson Memorial, Washington, D.C. (James Aycock)

home gardening out of which hundreds of garden clubs emerged across the land.

In 1956, President Dwight Eisenhower inaugurated the People-to-People programs which featured the *Sister City* concept. Interest in Japanese gardens and gardens of other countries increased. Today, there are over one hundred and six American cities that have adopted a sister city in Japan. Out of this exchange of ideas and national friendship have come the exchange of scholarships and meaningful gifts. Many of the Japanese gardens in America featured in this volume were gifts from a sister city in Japan.

Japanese flower arrangements especially received much attention from American gardeners and designers. *Ikebana* soon became a household word, synonymous with flower arrangements. Miniature trees, *bonsai;* and dish gardens, *bonkei* and *bonseki,* also were important terminologies in flower arrangements. Many books appeared which dealt exclusively with this special art, stimulating study courses and professional lectures.

The emphasis which is now placed on more easy-care American gardens undoubtedly stemmed from Japanese foundation planting that traditionally features rocks, sand and gravel, and clipped evergreens. Some of the loveliest residential areas in California and other southwestern states, and in Honolulu, display excellent examples of this adaptation of Japanese art designs.

Predominantly, however, it is a deep appreciation for the simplicity and beauty of these Oriental gardens which accounts for the many public and private Japanese gardens from coast to coast in America. Adaptations, of course, have been mandatory in some parts of the country because of climatic differences, availability of suitable plants and trees, and the special varieties of rocks required. Some of these "Japanese" gardens may seem rather strange to viewers who are steeped in traditions and rules for authentic Japanese gardening. But it has been said that "Imitation is the sincerest form of praise." In attempting to create Japanese gardens in so many parts of America, perhaps we are paying the highest tribute to the Japanese people and their fine art of gardening which so subtly expresses both beauty and tranquility of mind and spirit.

NOTES FOR TRAVELERS TO JAPAN

Any tour to Japan, however brief it may be, allows the visitor to see authentic Japanese gardens attached to palaces and temples, and in public parks. However, the Japan Travel Bureau does not provide "conducted garden tours" at this time (spring 1976). To arrange an individual tour to the finest gardens in any part of Japan, a book listed in our bibliography, *Invitation to Japanese Gardens,* is recommended. In addition to descriptions and text, there are superb color photographs and maps of special areas where choice gardens are open to visitors.

The most popular time for garden lovers to visit Japan, of course, is in the spring. Then the cherry trees are in bloom! In late October and November there is glorious color from the Japanese maples, and their unique chrysanthemum shows provide excitement and beauty since this is the time of competition displays. One of the largest attractions at these shows are the "flower dolls"—life-sized figures made of flowers, with lovely wax-character heads, and displayed in tableau settings. Each series of settings depict events in the life of an historical Japanese patriot or "hero." The kimonos which clothe these figures are made entirely from living chrysanthemums which have been placed in receptacles inside a wire or bamboo frame; the blossoms are then drawn through the meshes to create a colorful fabric-like effect.

The date and time when these dolls are to be displayed at chrysanthemum shows may be obtained by writing several weeks in advance to: The Japan Travel Bureau, Goyo Konsetsu Building, 1-12-1 Nihonbashi, Tokyo 103, Japan. You are sure to find their tourist service helpful and instructive, as well as expert in devising itineraries to please both individual and tour groups of any reasonable number.

Above, lotus design of garden beds at Jain Temple in Calcutta, India. (Charles Holman) Below, lower terraces of Pinjore gardens in Pinjore, India. (Punjab Agricultural University)

Formal Gardens
of India

*A garden is the purest of
human pleasures.*

EMPEROR BABUR
FOUNDER OF THE
MONGOL DYNASTY

An inscription, ordered by Emperor Asoka in the third century
b.c., which may still be seen on a pillar in Delhi, reads: "God's
beloved, Priyadarshi king, says to give shade to human beings and
quadrupeds—I have planted banyan and mango trees."

Trees were of great importance in ancient India, often the only
protection from constant scorching heat. The people yearned for
shade near their homes; and the owner of a house that possessed
such luxury was much envied. It is not surprising that tree worship
was a part of their religion dating as far back as 3000 B.C. For
centuries they were the subject of songs and poems sung or recited
at celebrations of special festivals. As early as 100-600 A.D.,
young women wore garlands of tree blossoms in their hair and
draped about their neck and arms as they danced. Wall paintings
attest to this in scenes found in the Ajanta caves.

Trees provided shelter, fruits and nuts for food, wood for
fashioning implements of peace and of war, and fuel to warm their
caves. But always, history and legend record, it was the beauty of
their flowers which excited the poetic Indian soul. Imagination
created symbolisms which ultimately became a part of Buddhist

rites. The fragrant yellow magnolia (*Michelia champaca*) was offered to Vishnu, god of procreation; blossoms from the orchid tree (*Bauhinia*) were sacred to Krishna. Many other trees indigenous to India have become known the world over—acacia, cassia, coral tree, and plumeria. Royal poinciana, familiarly known as *Flame of the Forest of India,* is found in exotic gardens of many gentle-climate countries. Almonds, oranges, plums, pomegranates and wild pears, believed to have originated in India, also now are grown in many areas where the climate is suitable.

Perhaps the earliest descriptions of gardens of India are those which appeared in the book, *Kamasutra,* written by Vatsayana about 300-400 A.D. Three kinds of palace gardens are mentioned: the first, and most luxurious, was for the enjoyment of the king and queen; a second was for the king's private use, recreation, playing chess, watching dancing girls and other entertainers; a third, for the pleasures of court officials and courtesans. This garden plan was traditional for many centuries.

Travelers to the *Jai Niwas* gardens which adjoin the palace in Jaipur are often shown the statue of a dog in one of the royal gardens, while a guide relates its story. Raja Jagat Singh, oppressed by the stifling heat of the palace, often escaped to some shady corner of his private garden. There he wrote love letters and poems to favorites of his harem, which his dog faithfully carried to each of the chosen maidens, bringing back to his master their replies. In tribute to the animal's devotion and intelligence, the Raja ordered the statue designed and placed in his private garden.

By the 12th-14th centuries, palace gardens were regarded as the most important feature of royal architectural design. Later, when hordes of conquerors invaded the country now known as India, each successive ruler chose a different site for the royal palace and government buildings.

The Mongol conquerors of a later period created the first real flower gardens in India—a concept they brought from Persia. Mongol palaces were planned to become the ruler's future tomb; thus, there were lavish gardens surrounding the palaces, and even within their mighty fortresses. Having come from mountainous countries, the conquering warriors could not appreciate India's rather flat gardens and constructed great mounds with many terraces, more characteristic of their native terrain. The number of terraces constructed also carried symbolic meanings. "Seven" represented the seven planets; "eight" signified the number of sanctuaries believed to await the faithful in paradise; "twelve," the twelve terraces for each sign of the Zodiac. In time, waterfalls and cascades were created to tumble down into pools and canals.

Those beautifully planted areas were divided into three general sections: the emperor's garden; the well-secluded ladies' garden; and areas reserved for the people's enjoyment. The cooling sounds of cascading waters could be heard throughout the landscaped grounds, providing a lullaby for those who sought relaxation from a noonday siesta. For others, there was the excitement of beauty in variations of water jets curving to meet, or to rise in flashing geysers high into the blue heavens, falling back in crystal baubles to float away on the rippling surface of the pool, creating new patterns from their reflections; or watching as underwater jets sent up soft bubbles to float like swans on a placid pool.

The perfume from flowers, surprisingly, was more appreciated by the Mongols than the beauty and color of the flower itself. Many courtyards were planted for nighttime fragrance and the pale loveliness of jasmine and tube-roses, romantically exotic in the soft light of myriad tiny oil lamps set into wall receptacles casting reflections onto the waters below.

Marble pavilions in every corner of these gardens provided for respite from the heat of noonday with cooling shadows. Occasionally a pavilion was constructed over running water near the center of the garden. Here a cool, refreshing breeze added to other comforts for relaxation. Another type of shelter, a "baridari," was a frequent part of the Mongols' gardens. This was a roofed structure, open on all sides and supported by pillars decorated with painted vases of flowers. These were used for enjoyment during the rainy season; for having suffered through months of scorching heat and hot winds, everyone reveled in the first torrents of heavy rains. Sitting comfortably in the baridaris, they could watch the great black clouds building up, then loosening their life-giving bounty upon the earth below; and feel the cooling winds on their faces. Most baridaris were comfortably furnished with thick carpets and cushions. Some were large enough to permit dancing girls for entertainment while the owner and guests partook of refreshment from ripe mangoes or other succulent fruits.

Traveling through India today, only remnants of these luxurious palaces and their walled gardens may be seen. But who among us can fail to clearly imagine those romantic gardens? Song and legend have made them an unforgettable part of our lives: the great ornate spaces, the turbaned throngs, perfumed ladies of the harems in exotic colorful silks and priceless brocades, adorned with equally priceless jewels. These were the living, colorful "flowers" that enlivened the mysterious gardens of old India, exquisitely extolled by Rimsky-Korsakov with his haunting melody in *The Song of India.*

NOTES FOR TRAVELERS TO INDIA

Almost every garden lover must have had a desire, at one time or another, to see the legendary splendors of the Taj Mahal, and Lahore's seventeenth century *Garden of Delights,* Shalamar. The latter is a vast complex, typical of the Mongol period, with enormous pools, pavilions and breathtaking cascades. It is a journey not to be missed.

In 1973, Shalamar was turned over to the Pakistan Department of Archaeology for restoration. It is now illumined at night to display its legendary grandeur. Another mecca, renowned in song and story, is the Vale of Kashmir with many beautiful gardens—a name that has become synonymous with beauty and romance.

One of the best sources of information on gardens in India is *Fodor's Guide,* published by David McKay Company. It includes descriptions of gardens at Humayun's tomb, the Pearl Mosque, and several others near Delhi; also fine gardens at Mandor near Jodhpur, and the palace gardens, *Jai Niwas,* at Jaipur. Others may be seen in Kashmir, Mysore and Calcutta.

The Public Relations Department of India Travel Service, Ltd. (60 E. 42nd St., New York, NY 10017) will send prospective travelers an extensive listing of the best-known gardens in various parts of that country, indicating the dates of maximum blooming. Also listed are botanical gardens, addresses of garden clubs, and places where flower shows may be seen annually. Some gardens on this list may be strongly influenced by British designs, somewhat more English than traditionally Indian.

Many of the garden books listed in our bibliography are recommended for study before setting forth on a journey to India.

Enchanted Gardens of Persia

Firdawsi, 1000 A.D.

Few descriptive phrases so vividly evoke fanciful dreams as does the simple term *Persian garden.* At once the reader is caught up in a vision of loveliness—exquisite young women in flowing garments strolling with devoted admirers along winding paths in an exotic garden perfumed by the fragrance of many flowers, or relaxing in small garden pavilions whose alabaster pillars are entwined with fragrant garlands.

Undoubtedly these enchanting gardens immortalized in song and story existed in ancient times, for historians have recorded them in authentic documents which confirm the importance and beauty of gardens in the life style of ancient Persia. Here, amidst perfumed loveliness, body and mind and spirit were restored to serenity through hours of quiet meditation and relaxation.

Persian gardens were believed to be true expressions of paradise—a foretaste of perfection that awaited the faithful after their earthly life had ended. The word *paradise* is Persian. Originally it was translated "park," for according to ancient descriptions it was "an enclosure around a residence." The first reference to paradise was found in a Greek manuscript by Xenophon, who wrote: "The

Persian King (Cyrus the Great) is well cared for, so that he may find gardens wherever he goes. Their name is Paradise, and they are full of all things fair and good that the earth can bring forth."

Later, when Cyrus and his conquering hordes reached the lands of the Mediterranean they admired the parks and gardens found in Babylonia and Assyria, but the geometrical enclosures of Egyptian gardens pleased them most of all. These they adapted and enlarged, creating vast complexes of "pleasure-grounds" about the palaces of Persia. The prevailing religion was Zoroastrianism. This belief extolled heavenly gardens filled with flowers and fruits and magnificent pavilions studded with precious jewels; and gave new meaning to the word *paradise.* In time, the name became synonymous with "a place of inexpressible beauty and luxury, reserved only for the Faithful."

Later, when the entire region along the Mediterranean came under Arab rule and the name of the country became Iran, Mohammedanism replaced Zoroastrianism (which is still practiced in that country), but the philosophy of paradise continued with greater emphasis; for the Koran heaven consists of seven paradises, five of them believed to be superlative gardens of inexpressible delights.

The Arabs governed Iran for more than four centuries, absorbing and adapting Persian designs and architectural features. Some of these were gradually submerged by changes growing out of differences in the way of life or the preference of a reigning ruler, but the Persian garden design survived more or less in its original purity. Eventually, when the expanding Arabian empire added Spain to its possessions, Persian gardens were introduced into courtyards surrounding the magnificent palaces once occupied by rulers and kings of Spain. A few of these have survived. In Granada, today, may be seen some of the finest examples of the Persian garden influence upon Spanish garden design. Here are the traditional "raised" pools, constructed in the shape of a cross, ornamented by fountains and surrounded by beds of colorful flowers, edged with potted plants which are changed during blossoming seasons. The tall cypresses and flowering trees which surround these gardens are also vivid examples of Persian influence, undoubtedly brought to Spain by Persian gardeners and architects and handed down from father to son. Every yellow rose, wherever grown today, is a descendant of cuttings sent to Spain at that time by the Shah of Persia.

Marco Polo's descriptions of Persian gardens as he first beheld them in 1300 A.D. are unquestionably the most authentic, and doubtlessly contributed the principles of design and ornamental details to descriptions by later writers. He tells us that Tamerlane, the great conqueror, delighted in creating gardens of unparalleled beauty which surrounded his magnificent palace at Samarkand. Some of these gardens were so vast that in one of them a workman was said to have lost his horse, which he finally found six months later!

Babur, the fifteenth-century conqueror who swept through Persia during his conquest of India, kept a diary which not only recorded his victorious battles and significant events of his government, but contained detailed descriptions of his palace gardens. Fortunately, the diary records were preserved and have contributed enormously to reconstructing valuable information about designs and plantings of gardens in Persia and India during that period. One of Babur's favorite gardens was the Degh-i-Vafa near Kabul. Frequently from his palace in India he sent instructions about new designs and the garden's upkeep, yet he did not revisit Degh-i-Vafa until fifteen years after its completion. Apparently his military conquests left him little time to enjoy the peaceful beauty of the gardens he had ordered constructed!

The pinnacle of Persian garden popularity was reached toward the end of the sixteenth century when Shah Abbas began building the new cities of Isfahan and Bushahr which strongly reflected the influence of Mohammedanism. Every mosque, school, public bath, hostelry and palace had its own garden, planned for both indoor and outdoor living. Many areas or "rooms" were open to the sky; others, partially or fully covered areas beside beautiful pools and canals, were planted with trees and flowers and ornamented by exquisite fountains.

The hot, arid plateaus upon which most Iranian towns and villages were built had a great need for water. Irrigation was vital to verdant growths and flowers, but the main source of water was from melted snow flowing down from the mountains.

The Persians solved the problem with an ingenious device called "qanat line" which is still used today. The first qanat line was built about 600 B.C. A master shaft was sunk to a depth of a hundred feet, if necessary, to reach the permanent water table at the base of a mountain, and at a point slightly higher than the desired destination of its feeder lines to take advantage of the slope. A tunnel was then dug, extending several hundred feet, or even miles, which could carry the water to every village and town. Near the population center, the qanat became an open canal, forming great pools which first supplied water to the qanat's owner; then, in turn, to users who bought various amounts. There was a "master of the water" in each village. It was his responsibility to rent out the channels, at specified times, to the small farmers and garden owners.

Considering the great difficulty in obtaining water for growing purposes, it is surprising that the palaces of even the earliest rulers of these lands were surrounded by garden areas which contained large pools.

In Persia, as in India where sun and hot winds prevail, the most demanding needs of rich or poor were for refreshing shade and cooling water. The pools of the wealthy were lined with colorful tiles and decorated by floating blossoms; illuminated at night by rows of candles set at recessed intervals in the surrounding walls. Small cascades flowed rhythmically from one level to another, bestowing refreshment of mind and spirit through both sight and sound during the sultry dry seasons. (Even today in modern Iran almost every home, large or small, has a pool in the courtyard.) The very wealthy built tile-lined beautiful pools in an inner courtyard adjacent to harem balconies. Other pools were lined with marble inlaid with precious stones which gleamed brightly through the crystal waters. One erotic nineteenth century Shah was said to have constructed spacious pools in his inner palace courtyards which provided marble chutes from the harem balconies down which his favorites could slide, naked, to disport themselves for hours in the refreshing water for his private entertainment.

The pools of the poor at first were never more than a rectangular tank such as was used in India. But the Persians' love of decoration even here often asserted itself. Pools were soon built in a variety of shapes; some with scalloped edges resembling a flower, others irregular in outline with curves and triangles. Flowers filled the outer edges.

Persian palace gardens, under Mongolian rule, underwent various changes in design. The small pavilions, which traditionally were placed at each corner of a Persian garden, were sophisticated versions of Mongol tent shelters. At the center of each courtyard garden stood a taller pavilion, doubtlessly reserved for royal usage. The interior of each pavilion was elaborately furnished and decorated with priceless vases of fragrant flowers and other cherished artifacts, most of which also were enormously valuable. Prisms and brightly colored stalactite objects hung from a domed ceiling, glittering when swayed by the gentle movements of cooling winds. Walls were covered by richly colored murals which extolled the pleasures of paradise, or victorious exploits of the reigning ruler. But the walls of special pavilions reserved for erotic dalliance were completely surfaced with intricate mirror-mosaics of unusual origin. Mirrors for all palaces were imported from Europe and, having endured long journeys by ships and caravans, frequently arrived in somewhat shattered condition. Crafty Persian artisans made rewarding uses of these rejected shards by creating exquisite designs with which to decorate pavilion walls and ceilings. Here, in privacy and luxurious comfort, sheltered from sun and wind, hours of pleasurable indulgence might be spent with favorites of court or harem.

In northern Iran, the brief spring brings a blaze of color. Wild flowers of many hues carpet the valleys. Blossoming trees—almond, apricot and plum—perfume the air. Gardens overflow with flowers of the season in lavish displays of anemones, narcissus, hyacinths, pinks and violets. Emperor Babur, in his diary, mentions thirty-two different varieties of short, brilliant "species" tulips. But the favorite, and Persia's national flower, is the rose. As early as the eleventh century, history records "a hundred-petaled rose." Tree roses of great age and size bordered pools, shedding fragrance upon every garden; for while the rose's beauty has been acclaimed in Persia for centuries in verse and song, its fragrance is most prized. *Attar of Roses* perfume, symbol of perfection, pays tribute to Persia's national flower. Gardeners throughout the world also pay tribute to this lovely fragrance—for no flower garden, great or small, ever is complete until its roses are in bloom!

Beautiful and useful orchards adjoined every Persian garden's pools and flowerbeds. The citrus fruits, especially the orange, had been introduced into Persia from China long before the Arab conquerors arrived. Apples, pears, plums, and apricots provided fruit throughout the centuries. Later, the peach, cherry and fig also were introduced. These large areas adjacent to the flower gardens added their own heavy fragrance to the air, and furnished delectable fruits for their owners and guests.

While Persian gardens, immortalized by legend and song, may command first attention from all lovers of gardens, little has been said about the orchards which usually adjoined floral gardens even in earliest times, although their fruits are frequently praised. These vast orchards were usually framed by tall cypress and plane trees which formed dense hedges.

Small aviaries and zoos also had their special places in royal Persian gardens and in gardens of the wealthy. Here peacocks of stately jewel-like grandeur freely strutted about the spacious grounds. Shy gazelles roamed adjoining fields, the epitome of grace and gentleness. Much of this delicate beauty has been preserved in exquisite miniatures and paintings which are now collectors' treasures. Persia's famous carpets, long appreciated for superb craftsmanship and richness of color and design, have inspired designers of gardens, a few of whom have reproduced the luxurious patterns with growing garden flowers, showing cross-pools, pavilions, trees and flowers in exact detail.

It is unfortunate that Western influence during the twentieth century has tragically obliterated most of the great traditional gardens of Persia. Many of their ancient buildings, however, have been carefully preserved and still are viewed with awe by travelers to that country. Apparently little effort has been made toward recreating the wonders of their ancient gardens, perhaps of even greater interest to many visitors.

NOTES FOR TRAVELERS TO PERSIA

Among the truly traditional old gardens of Persia still to be seen, we suggest the following:

Chehel Sotun in Isafahan, also known as the Hall of the Forty Columns, is so named because its twenty columns are so perfectly reflected in the garden's pool. The building was erected by Shah

By Maurice Shadbolt

Who Killed the Bog Men of Denmark? And Why?

EVERY YEAR in the Danish town of Silkeborg, thousands of visitors file past the face of a murder victim. No one will ever know his name. It is enough to know that 2000 years ago he was as human as ourselves. That face has moved men and women to poetry, and to tears.

Last summer I journeyed to the lake-girt Danish town and, peering at that face behind glass in a modest museum, I felt awe—for his every wrinkle and whisker tell a vivid and terrible tale from Denmark's distant past. The rope which choked off the man's breath is still around his neck. Yet it is a perplexingly peaceful face, inscrutable, one to haunt the imagination.

This strangest of ancient murder mysteries began 27 years ago, on May 8, 1950, when two brothers, Emil and Viggo Højgaard, were digging peat in Tollund Fen, near Silkeborg. Their spring sowing finished, the brothers were storing up the umber-

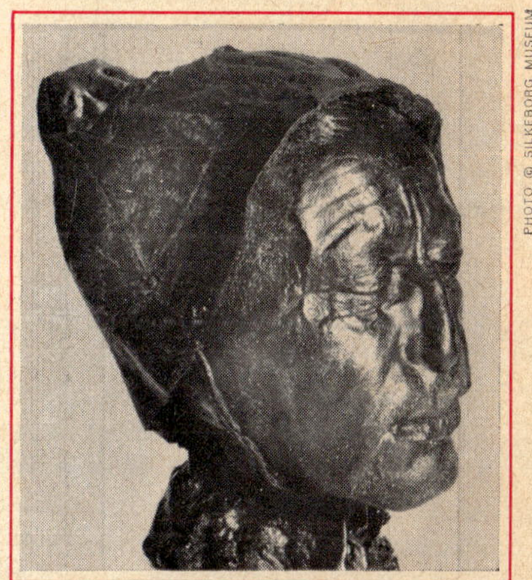

The hauntingly serene face of Tollund man, who died 2000 years ago

brown peat for their kitchen range, and for warmth in the winter to come. It was a peaceful task on a sunny morning. Snipe called from the aspens and firs fringing the dank bowl of the fen, where only heather and coarse grass grew. Then, at a depth of nine feet, their spades suddenly struck something.

They were gazing, with fright and fascination, at a face underfoot. The corpse was naked but for a skin cap, resting on its side as if asleep, arms and legs bent. The face was gentle, with eyes closed and lips lightly pursed. There was stubble on the chin. The bewildered brothers called the Silkeborg police.

Quick to the scene, the police did not recognize the man as anyone listed missing. Shrewdly guessing the brothers might have blundered into a black hole in Europe's past, the police called in archeologists.

Enter Prof. Peter Glob, a distinguished scholar from nearby Aarhus University, who carefully dislodged a lump of peat from beside the dead man's head. A rope made of two twisted hide thongs encircled his neck. He had been strangled or hanged. But when, and by whom? Glob ordered a box to be built about the corpse and the peat in which it lay, so nothing might be disturbed.

Next day, the box, weighing nearly a ton, was manhandled out of the bog onto a horse-drawn cart, on its way for examination at Copenhagen's National Museum. One of Glob's helpers collapsed and died with the huge effort. It seemed a

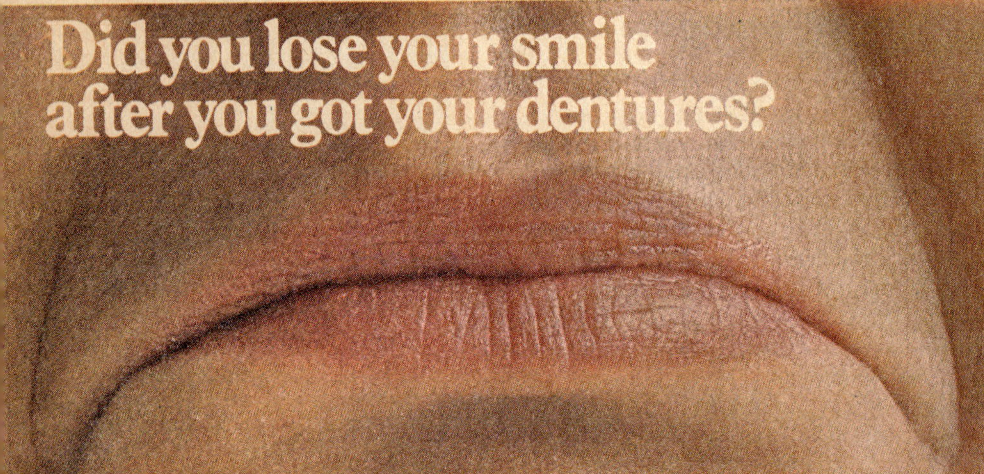

It's pretty tough to smile when you're worried about dingy, yellow dentures. Dentu-Creme has an anti-yellowing formula that gets rid of dingy yellow film that can make dentures look unnatural.

In fact, with regular use, Dentu-Creme can help keep the yellow from coming back. **It gives you back your smile.**

dark omen, as if some old god were claiming a modern man in place of a man from the past.

Bog bodies were nothing new—since records have been kept, Denmark's bogs have surrendered no fewer than 400—and the preservative qualities of the humic acid in peat have long been known. But not until the 19th century did scientists and historians begin to glimpse the finds and understand that the bodies belonged to remote, murky recesses of European prehistory. None survived long: the corpses were either buried again or crumbled quickly with exposure to light and air.

When peat-digging was revived during and after World War II, bodies were unearthed in abundance—first in 1942 at Store Arden, then in 1946, 1947 and 1948 at Borre Fen. Artifacts found beside them positively identified them as people of Denmark's Early Iron Age, from 400 B.C. to A.D. 400. None, then, was less than 1500 years old, and some were probably much older. The first of the Borre Fen finds—a full-grown male—was to prove especially significant: Borre Fen man, too, had died violently, with a noose about his neck, strangled or hanged. And his last meal had consisted of grain.

Peter Glob, alongside his artist father (a portraitist and distinguished amateur archeologist), had been digging into Denmark's dim past since he was a mere eight years old. For him, the Tollund man, who had by far the best-preserved head to

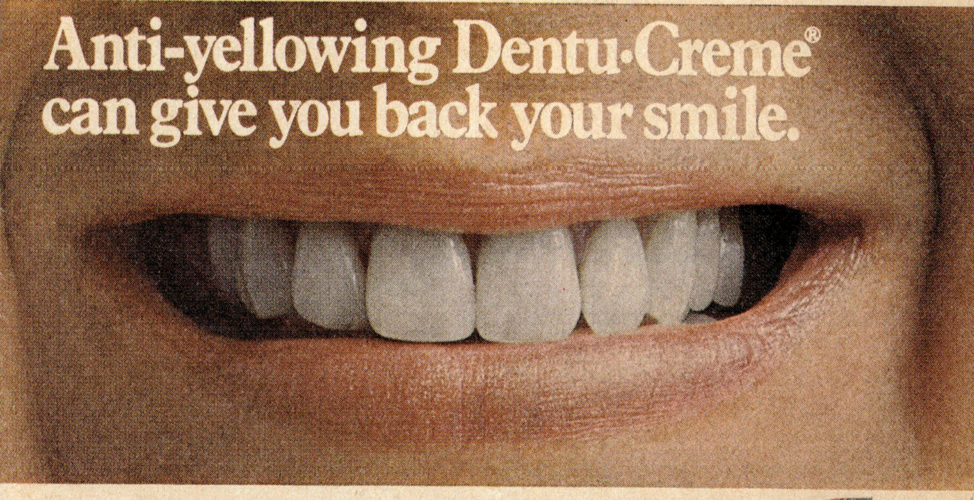

survive from antiquity, was a supreme challenge. Since 1936, Glob had been living imaginatively with the pagan hunters and farmers of 2000 years ago, fossicking among their corroded artifacts, foraging among the foundations of their simple villages; he knew their habits, the rhythms of their lives. Suddenly, here was a man of that very time. "Majesty and gentleness," he recalls, "seemed to stamp his features as they did when he was alive." What was this enigmatic face trying to tell him?

Glob was intrigued by the fact that so many of the people found in bogs had died violently: strangled or hanged, throats slit, heads battered. Perhaps they had been travelers set upon by brigands, or executed criminals. But there might be a different explanation. These murder victims all belonged to the Danish Iron Age. If they were to be explained away as victims of robber bands, there should be a much greater spread in time—into other ages. Nor would executed criminals all have had so many common traits.

Glob considered the body with care. X rays of Tollund man's vertebrae, taken to determine whether he had been strangled or hanged, produced inconclusive results. The condition of the wisdom teeth suggested a man well over 20 years old. An autopsy revealed that the heart, lungs and liver were well preserved; most important, the alimentary canal was undisturbed, containing the dead man's last meal—a 2000-year-

old gruel of hand-milled grains and seeds: barley, linseed, flaxseed, knotgrass, among others. Knowledge of prehistoric agriculture made it possible to determine that the man had lived in the first 200 years A.D. The mixture of grains and seeds suggested a meal prepared in winter or early spring.

Since Iron Age men were not vegetarians, why were there no traces of meat? Glob also marveled that the man's hands and feet were soft; he appeared to have done little or no heavy labor in his lifetime. Possibly, then, he was high-ranking in Iron Age society.

Then, on April 26, 1952, peat-digging villagers from Grauballe, 11 miles east of Tollund, turned up a second spectacularly well-preserved body, and again Glob was fast to the scene. Unmistakably another murder victim, this discovery was, unlike Tollund man, far from serene. The man's throat had been slashed savagely from ear to ear. His face was twisted with terror, and his lips were parted with a centuries-silenced cry of pain.

Glob swiftly removed the body— still imbedded in a great block of peat—for preservation and study. Carbon-dating of body tissue proved Grauballe man to be about 1650 years old, a contemporary of Constantine the Great. Grauballe man was in extraordinary condition; his fingerprints and footprints came up clearly. Tallish and dark-haired, Grauballe man, like Tollund man, had never done any heavy manual

BUY-WORDS *from Carolyn*

All too often, as you're enjoying a summer day outdoors, you discover unwelcome company: Poison ivy, oak and sumac. But they don't have to spoil your family's good times—not when you can keep **Ivy-Dry** on hand. For over 25 years, safe, effective Ivy-Dry has been relieving the itching and blisters caused by poisonous plants. It also soothes the discomfort of sunburn, insect bites and minor skin irritations. Both children and adults can use Ivy-Dry with safety and confidence. So be prepared before someone runs into poison ivy, oak or sumac: You get **Ivy-Dry** lotion or cream wherever fine drug products are sold.

Just as people feel better after a good bath on a hot day, so does a dog: Your pet not only looks and smells better when you shampoo him regularly in summer, but he's happier, too. And he'll be even happier when you choose any fine shampoo from Sergeant's® wide variety. **Skip-Flea® Shampoo** (in both 8 oz. and economy 12 oz. sizes) cleans, deodorizes, kills fleas and lice. For a long-haired dog, **Anti-Tangle Shampoo's** special conditioners help prevent tangling and matting. An extra luxurious formula, **Sergeant's Creme Shampoo** gives the coat high luster. You can always rely on Sergeant's.

You may love spending lots of time in the sunshine, but the result may not be good for your skin: It can become dry and tight. **Desitin Skin Care** moisturizes summertime skin, leaving it fresh, soft, smooth feeling. Its rich formula helps relieve tightness and smoothes away dry, peeling skin. Desitin Skin Care is richer in skin softeners than any other leading lotion, yet absorbs quickly without greasiness. You can get this great skin care two ways: Regular Desitin Skin Care in the yellow bottle with a hint of fragrance, or **Baby Fresh Desitin Skin Care** in the blue bottle, a real baby powder scent.

After a few months your puppy's outsides may look full grown. But if you could see your puppy's insides, you'd see how his bones and muscles continue to grow and develop for a full year. That's why—for a full year—a puppy needs extra protein, calcium and other nutrients. The kind he gets in **Purina Puppy Chow**—the special formula puppy food. With Purina Puppy Chow you can be sure that your puppy gets all the nutrition he needs for full internal development. So feed your puppy **Purina Puppy Chow** — for a full year—to be sure that his insides catch up with his outsides.

When summer days have you saying, "It's too hot to cook," you can still enjoy a flavorful, satisfying meal without heating up the kitchen—if you have **Campbell's Chunky Soup** on hand. Here's one menu to try soon: For the main course, Chunky Split Pea with Ham Soup—with chunk after chunk of ham, plus carrots, potatoes and celery in a puree of cooked split peas, all deliciously blended to bring out that home-style flavor. Serve with salad, buttered rolls and milk. For variety, try Chunky Sirloin Burger Soup. **Campbell's Chunky Soups** make your summer mealtimes easier and more enjoyable.

Canker sores can be painful, as you know, if anyone in your family has had them. Cank-aid™, with its healing oxygen formula, can help you eat, drink and be free from the miseries of canker sores four ways: 1) Helps relieve pain. 2) Helps soothe inflammation and irritation. 3) Helps cleanse canker sores. 4) Helps wash away food particles where bacteria and odor breed. And Cank-aid is so easy to use. Just a few drops from the painless no-touch tip applicator helps provide you with soothing relief. **Cank-aid** is available without prescription at drug stores everywhere.

Shopping for the season's fresh fruits and vegetables, how do you get the best produce for your money? Here are some pointers: 1. Be sure pre-packaged carrots, spinach, potatoes and onions don't look wet; one spoiled vegetable or leaf can rapidly ruin the rest. 2. The juiciest citrus fruits weigh the most. Choose lemons, oranges and grapefruit that are heavy for their size. 3. A ripe pear, peach, melon, tomato or avocado should yield slightly to a gentle touch, but still feel firm. You can ripen some fruits at room temperature at home: A grocer who wants your business can give you good advice.

For a hot weather treat children love, add a scoop or two of vanilla ice cream to a glass of cold grape juice. Serve with a straw. (It's called a "purple cow.")

work. He had been slain in his late 30s. Another similarity came to light when Grauballe man's last meal was analyzed: it had been eaten immediately before death and, like Tollund man's, like Borre Fen man's too, it was a gruel of grains and seeds, a meal of winter, or early spring. All three had perished in a similar season.

Who had killed these men of the bogs? Why in winter, or early spring? Why should they—apparently—have led privileged lives? And why the same kind of meals before their sudden ends?

The bodies had told Glob all they could. Now he turned to one of his favorite sources—the Roman historian Tacitus. Nearly 2000 years ago Tacitus recorded the oral traditions of Germanic tribes who inhabited northwest Europe. Tacitus' account of these wild, brave and generous blue-eyed people often shed light into dark corners of Denmark's past. Glob found these lines: "At a time laid down in the distant past, all peoples that are related by blood meet in a sacred wood. Here they celebrate their barbarous rites with a human sacrifice."

Elsewhere, Tacitus wrote: "These people are distinguished by a common worship of Nerthus, or Mother Earth. They believe that she interests herself in human affairs." Tacitus confirmed early spring as a time among the Germanic tribes for offerings and human sacrifice. They were asking the goddess to hasten the coming of spring, and the summer harvest. Men chosen for sacrifice might well have been given a symbolic meal, made up of plant seeds, before being consecrated through death to the goddess—thus explaining the absence of meat. The sacrificial men, with their delicate features, neat hands and feet, might have been persons of high rank chosen by lot for sacrifice, or priests, ritually married to Nerthus.

Tacitus supplied another essential clue: the symbol of Nerthus, he recorded, was a twisted metal "torque," or neck ring, worn by the living to honor the goddess. The leather nooses about the necks of Tollund man and the body from Borre Fen and some earlier bodies were replicas of those neck rings. Glob concluded that it was Nerthus—Mother Earth herself—who had preserved her victims perfectly in her peaty bosom long after those who had fed them into the bogs were dust.

Peter Glob was satisfied. He had found the killer and identified the victims. The centuries-old mystery of Denmark's bog bodies was no more.

Classified Classics

FROM THE SAN JOSE, CALIF., *Sun:* "WANTED: One old worn-out saddle for one small boy to daydream on."

FROM THE "HELP WANTED" SECTION of a Missouri newspaper: "We're packing them in nightly at the Royal Banquet! Get a second-shift job! Apply personnel office, Royal Banquet Sardine Cannery."

GARAGE-SALE AD in the Asheville, N.C., *Citizen-Times:* "Recently married couple must consolidate two complete households. All duplicates (except children) must be sold."

NOTICE in the Perry County, Pa., *Times:* "An escaped shovel from the Shope Sawmill. Would the person who helped it escape please see that it is returned? Its sentence of hard labor is not complete!"

FOR-SALE AD in the New Smyrna Beach, Fla., *News & Observer:* "Lady's gym suit, size 42 large. Also badly bent gym set."

Baby Talk. Donald Ogden Stewart, the writer, had a son away at prep school. When the boy reached the age of 14, Stewart wrote him the following letter: "Dear Son: Now that you have reached the magic age of 14, the time has come to tell you about the bees and flowers. There is a male bee and a female bee, although I haven't the slightest idea which is which. As for the flowers—we get ours from the Plaza Florists, Inc. Well, that takes care of *that.* Write soon. Affectionately, Father."

Abbas II in 1647, and for centuries was used for official occasions. Both the building and its garden are being restored.

At Shiraz, the charming pavilion of Kolah Parangi, which may be seen at the Pars Museum, is beautifully decorated with tiles and floral paintings. Its octagonal marble basin is constructed from one piece of marble, with a fountain in its center. The small fortress of Arg-E-Karim-Khani, also at Shiraz, is a fascinating complex of buildings and gardens. Parts of the "Orange Garden" (Bagh-E-Delgosha) in the same city are very lovely (as shown in the photograph on page 48) but other areas have suffered from modernization. The Garden of Bagh-E-Eram is probably the best known to tourists visiting Shiraz. Some of its magnificent cypress trees attain a height of forty-five feet. Both the buildings and the gardens are faithful to old Persian tradition.

On the road from Shiraz to Qasrod-Dasht (about 2 kilometers from Shiraz) is a very lovely garden of flowerbeds, pools, and an orchard of pomegranates called Afifabad, which is well worth visiting. As a final stop in Shiraz—and not to be missed—is the exquisite garden at the new Asian Institute building, Narenjestan, formerly of private ownership but now remodeled at the suggestion of Empress Farah Pahlavi.

In Tehran, the gardens of the Golestan Palace are especially lovely and their pavilions show excellent examples of the unique mirror-mosaic art which was used extensively in earlier times.*

Prospective visitors to Persia certainly should obtain a copy of the paperback book, *Iran Today* (illustrated in color, priced at $5.00; obtainable from the Iran Information and Tourist Center, 10 West 49th St., New York, NY 10020). For a comprehensive history of the gardens of Persia, Wilber's beautiful volume, mentioned in the bibliography, is heartily recommended. The beauty of the gardens of the Shah Abbas Hotel in Isfanhan is legendary among travelers.

When planning an itinerary it would heighten the traveler's interest to make a point of being in Persia on the first day of spring, March 21, to witness the annual "New Year" festival which lasts thirteen days. Until fairly recently, every family celebrated

---

*We are indebted to Mr. Mohammed Ghaissari of Tehran for the foregoing information, taken from his thesis on "The Persian Garden; Its Origin and Development."

by decorating a *haft sin* table with arrangements of seven special flowers—a tradition dating from the Zoroastrian period. A copy of the Koran placed in front of a mirror completed this sacred table ceremony. The original flowers used were myrtle, jasmine, forget-me-not, sweet basil, pussywillow, lily-of-the-valley, and either a lily or an iris. More recently, due to a diminishing supply of some of these flowers, branches of seven sacred trees were substituted. Today, the arrangement usually consists of apple, sumac, a dish of green vegetables, a pot of hyacinths, medlar fruit (*Mespilus germanica*), vinegar, and a dish of germinating wheat or malt mixed with flour.

"Orange Garden" in Shiraz, Iran. (Iran Information & Tourism Center)

Part Two

A Guide to Oriental Gardens in America

Invitation to America's Oriental Gardens

This collection of public Oriental gardens in America, assembled here for the first time, offers a fascinating variety of beauty in plants, flowers, and settings, and in unusual designs.

Most of these gardens are located in public parks or botanical gardens. Others may be found at universities, museums, motels, restaurants and business buildings. One was discovered next to a dentist's office! A few are of Indo-Persian design or a blending of various Oriental themes.

The stories about origins and development of Oriental gardens in America are equally varied, but it is significant that each came into being because of the enthusiasm and vision of one individual who desired to share this form of beauty with other Americans. The achievement of such goals, of course, required much more than wishful thinking, for planting and designing and continuous care of growing plants take patience and persistence. Many local organizations, civic and commercial, cooperated in the creation of these gardens and, in working with Oriental-American citizens toward a cherished goal, formed new and lasting friendships.

Hotei, God of Prosperity and Happiness, in Miami. (Miami-Metro Department of Publicity and Tourism)

A number of the gardens presented here which are gifts from Japan or Japanese sister cities are beautiful examples of the innate generosity of the Japanese people. A few are Japanese gardens given to America by Americans in tribute to the inspirational beauty of Japanese landscape design.

These stories of garden origin and design are told in more detail in the descriptions of individual gardens.

Many garden lovers appreciate the symbolism to be found in Oriental garden designs and various ornamental objects. This is a study in itself, well worth pursuing, although only touched upon here as space permitted.

Each garden described herein has its own kind of memorable beauty. Whether visited in person or seen through the illustrations and text of this book, each will bestow upon the viewer a deep sense of serenity as enduring as the viewer's capacity to receive.

Alabama

Birmingham

Japanese Gardens in Birmingham Botanical Gardens

There is a wonderful feeling of continuity, of spaciousness, in these tranquil Japanese gardens which flow gradually into each other. Since they cover an area of 7½ acres, with undulating terrain, there are always new views at a distance as well as close by.

Perhaps this sense of perspective is due to the background of the designer, landscape architect Buffy Murai. Though born in San Francisco, he lived in Tokyo for twenty years, absorbing the

Plan of Japanese gardens. (Birmingham Botanical Gardens)

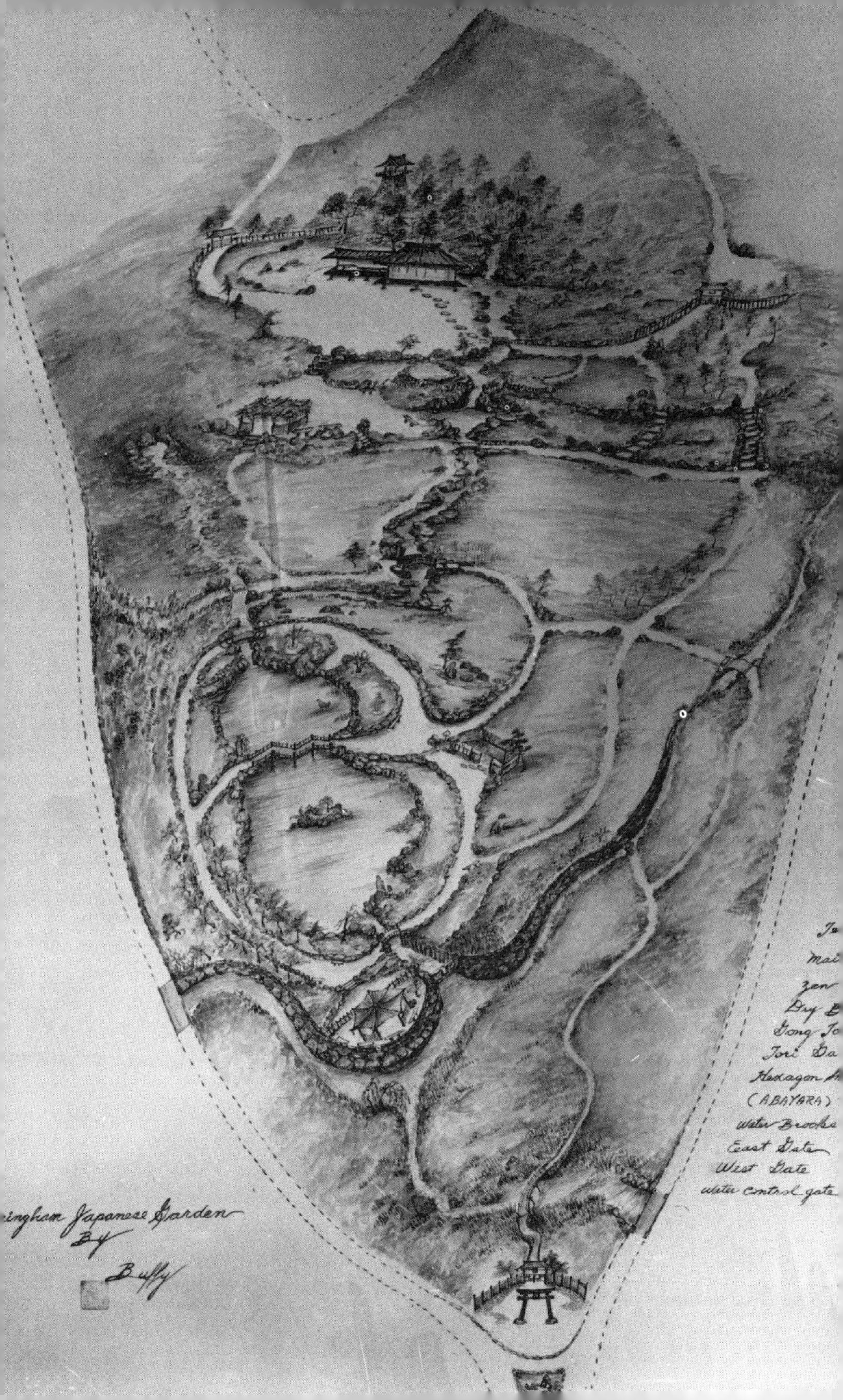

Jo
mai
zen
Dry B
Gong To
Tori Ga
Hexagon M
(ABAYARA)
Water Brooks
East Gate
West Gate
Water control gate
...ingham Japanese Garden
By
Buffy

traditions of Japanese garden art there. Then in America he became a motion picture set designer, acquiring fame with his scenes for *Around the World in Eighty Days,* and *Sayonara.* He has also been art director of the Cherry Blossom Festival in Washington. The gardens he designed for Birmingham were conceived like a series of stage sets, each representing a facet of Japan's ancient traditions to induce meditation, communion with nature, and quiet philosophical thought. Formal dedication took place in 1967 with Japanese Ambassador Ryuji Takeuch officiating.

After entering through the large *torii,* (gateway to heaven) the first garden on the left is the Zen Meditation Garden. The rocks placed in a "sea" of sand may mean different things to each viewer. Perhaps they are islands in an ocean, or mountains surrounded by clouds. Those who have studied Japanese interpretations may see the opposing forces called "Yin" and "Yang," or man and woman, fire and water, sun and moon. It is a garden for "mind expansion."

The path leads on from here over river gravel, dry much of the time, but ready to control the water resulting from sudden heavy rains. Here and there are symbolic stones, like the "Dragon's Head" which stares up from the ground. Nearby are trees pruned in the Japanese manner to represent layers of "clouds" at each branch level. The steps of the "Waterfalls of the Seven Virtues" signify faith, hope, charity, patience, temperance, fortitude and justice—as opposed to the seven deadly sins. The water flows from east to west, a good omen to the Japanese. In the lake is a turtle rock, which stands for longevity, thus giving the water its name of Long Life Lake. Another island is planted with flowers for the four seasons. Nearby is a "cooling breeze shelter" with fan-shaped openings on the side walls to allow the lake-cooled air to flow through.

Crossing the lake is the "Bridge of Accomplishment," a typical zigzag bridge denoting life's variety, or in older Japanese tradition, safety in crossing if pursued by evil spirits which can only go in a straight line. Another bridge beyond is a "moon bridge," sometimes called the "Circle of Life" with its completing reflection. The lovely teahouse on the hill was given to Birmingham by the Japanese government after it had been exhibited at the 1965 New York World's Fair. The solemn tea ceremony is demonstrated here on Sunday afternoons in spring and fall. A statue of Kuan Yin,

Irregular bridge. (Birmingham Botanical Gardens)

Goddess of Mercy, stands nearby. There are some 1800 azaleas scattered throughout the gardens, and thirty varieties of Japanese cherries, adding discreet spots of color among great areas of peaceful green.

OPEN: Daily, sunrise to sunset.

ADMISSION: Free.

ADDRESS: 2612 Lane Park Rd., Birmingham, AL 35223. Telephone: 205-879-1227, or 205-879-1576.

MAINTAINED BY: Birmingham Park and Recreation Board.

DIRECTIONS: From interchange of routes 31, 75 and Interstate 20, take Old Highway 280 south and follow garden signs.

Theodore

Oriental-American Garden—Bellingrath Gardens

This Oriental-American garden is a fairly recent addition to the fabled Bellingrath Gardens, renowned for their magnificent displays of azaleas and camellias. Approximately five acres were set aside in 1967 to provide this delightful Oriental section, designed by John M. Brown and Harry F. Ryan.

Five ponds of varied sizes—with water courses, curved bridges and waterfalls, artistically placed—set a peaceful meditative mood. Stately swans glide majestically about the ponds. A variety of talkative ducks enliven their parts of the pond with a pleasantly noisy friendliness. Flocks of brilliantly plumaged flamingos decorate quiet pools.

The dark wood used for buildings lend an ancient Oriental air. Lanterns of stone and cast iron, carefully placed, add a more diverse note, accented by reflections in pools and streams. A small structure with moon-shaped windows, positioned behind a red-railed bridge, creates a mystic picture in the water below (see color plate). An amusing feature is captured in the miniature Mount Fujiyama, about ten feet tall, its lower slopes covered with *Othiopogan japonica,* representing trees, and a "snow cap" of white sand.

The entire garden is significantly Oriental-American, combining both East and West in plantings and architecture; creating a place of great charm which has become a favorite spot for visitors to Bellingrath Gardens.

OPEN: Bellingrath Gardens are open daily from 7 a.m. to dusk. The Bellingrath Home is open from 8:30 a.m., with the last tour beginning at 4 p.m.

ADMISSION FEE: $2.40 for adults; $1.20 for children 6 to 11; free under age 6. Admission to the home: $3.00 per person.

ADDRESS: Bellingrath Gardens, Route 1, Box 60, Theodore, AL 36582. Telephone: 205-973-2217.

DIRECTIONS: Take US-90 southwest of Mobile or Interstate 10 to Theodore, then south on S-59. Ask Gray Line bus about tours from Mobile.

The Oriental-American Garden in Bellingrath Gardens. (Photos by Houston L. Baker)

Tuscaloosa

Japanese Garden of Gulf States Paper Corporation

The Japanese Garden surrounds the fantastic Oriental buildings of the national headquarters of the Gulf States Paper Corporation, which has branches throughout the South and East. The whole complex is the culmination of the dreams of its president and chairman of the board, Jack Warner. His travels and artistic interests had envisioned industrial buildings which would be beautiful as well as functional, with a restful, airy Oriental atmosphere within, and the beauty of Japanese garden vistas from every window.

The architectural plans were already set when a well-known landscape architect was brought in to design the gardens. This was David H. Engel, who had spent several years apprenticed to the master landscape architect of Kyoto, Tansai Sano, as the first American recipient of a Japanese Ministry of Education grant to study landscape architecture in Japan. He knew that this Alabama garden had to be related to the practical uses of a corporate office, with a simple design which would result in interesting vistas from all sides, as well as allow for passage between the many buildings. He also felt that the gardens should relate to the formation of the land, and that in a hot southern climate the inclusion of a waterfall and pond were important to give a dynamic, fresh feeling. In order to be characteristic of Japanese garden design, the many rocks were imported from Connecticut, but were chosen for emotional response and a natural effect rather than for any abstract symbolism so foreign to Americans.

Trees and shrubs were selected for the climate, but are all similar to those used in Japan, and are kept well clipped to preserve the original proportions of the design. The pavement of the forecourt, though of Tennessee sandstone, was cut to recreate an irregular Oriental design reminiscent of the Katsura Imperial Villa in Kyoto. All the stone lanterns were imported from Japan, one having a bas-relief of the Virgin Mary carved by early Japanese Christians. A thirteen-story stone pagoda makes a dramatic accent. A zigzag bridge leads to an island of irregular shape.

(Photos by Gulf States Paper Corporation)

Special lighting enhances the landscape at night. The garden might be called a Japanese stroll garden, since one can walk all around it on paths and balconies; but it also has the effectiveness of the home landscape gardens of Japan, since each view from a different window or building has been carefully planned for beauty. The grand opening on May 11, 1970, was attended by hundreds of specially invited VIPs including Ambassador Nobuhiko Ushiba of Japan and his cultural attaché, Mrs. Taeko Shima. The gardens and buildings together create an extraordinary restful Oriental atmosphere, unique for an American functional business office.

OPEN: Weekdays 5-8 p.m., Sat. 10 a.m. to 7 p.m. with tours on the hour; Sun. 1:30 p.m. to 7:30 p.m., tours on the half-hour. For tours, telephone 205-553-5831, or write Gulf States Paper Corp., P.O. Box 3199, Tuscaloosa, AL 35401. These include the grounds, the buildings, and the splendid art collection.

ADDRESS: Gulf States Paper Corp., 1400 River Rd., Tuscaloosa, AL 35401.

Arizona

Carefree

Japanese-type Garden at Carefree Inn

This large, pleasant motel has an extremely interesting Japanese-type garden on sloping, undulating terrain. Since it is in a desert setting, the basic principles of Japanese garden design were adapted very intelligently by using cacti and succulents as plants instead of evergreens. This is an example of how the Japanese garden design, and the feeling of space and tranquility, can be achieved in a very different climate. The garden is in a "U" shape, covering about 3/4 of an acre between two of the motel buildings. It was completed in 1963 by Andre's Nursery in Carefree.

The Japanese-type garden at Carefree Inn. (George Taloumis)

OPEN: All year. Rated "excellent" by the AAA.

ADDRESS: On Mule Train Rd., one-fourth mile north of Cave Creek Rd. Mail: Carefree Inn, P.O. Box 708, Carefree, AZ 85331. Telephone: 602-836-8711.

California

Auburn

Esther Baker Memorial Garden

The Esther Baker Memorial Garden, located in the patio of the Auburn-Placer Library, was created by the Auburn Garden Club in 1973 with funds from a bequest by a deceased member. The garden is named for her as a memorial; special plants will be added in memory of other deceased members.

It is a Japanese garden, designed by Mr. Ray Yamasaki, who continues to advise the club on the garden's care and new plantings. The traditional Japanese water basin here has now found a new use: the water which flows into its stone hollow from a bamboo pipe has become an attraction as a birdbath. This is touchingly appropriate as Esther Baker was an ardent bird lover.

OPEN: Only during library hours, as entrance to the garden is through the library.

A corner of the Esther Baker Memorial Garden, showing the water basin. (Rufus Hammond)

ADMISSION: Free.

ADDRESS: Auburn-Placer Library, 350 Nevada St., Auburn, CA 95603. Telephone: 916-823-4391.

Culver City

Kaizuka Meditation Garden

This charming Japanese garden is the gift of Culver City's Japanese Sister City, Kaizuka. It was a thank-you for the hospitality shown by Culver City's residents for more than twelve years to traveling Kaizuka athletes, Olympic officials and Kaizuka dignitaries.

Planned and fully constructed by engineers in Japan, all the garden's features were then dismantled and sent to Culver City for assembly. A bridge and rocks, weighing up to twelve tons each, were shipped to America and put in place by the men who had made or selected them. The most interesting object of all—rarely seen in Japanese gardens in America—was the wooden waterwheel. Appropriate trees and shrubs were supplied locally. The little pond is bright with the flashing colors of *koi* (carp). Many of the blue stones, the stone bridge and the Teshoku candleholder stone came from Shikoku Kochi prefecture, as did the colored gravel. The garden is enhanced by special lighting at night.

Kaizuka Meditation Garden was dedicated in April, 1974, in an authentic Japanese ceremony with a Shinto priest officiating. The mayor and eight officials of service clubs from Kaizuka were present.

OPEN: Daily.

ADMISSION: Free.

ADDRESS: The garden is at Culver City Library, 4975 Overland Ave., Culver City, CA 90230.

MAINTAINED BY: Culver City Department of Parks and Recreation, 4117 Overland Blvd., Culver City, CA 90230. Telephone: 213-837-5211.

Kaizuka Meditation Garden in Culver City. (Pacific Telephone Company)

El Cerrito

Persian Rug Garden

There is certainly no other garden like this in America! It covers an entire steep hillside, with brilliant flowers designed as a series of Persian carpets and an old-fashioned quilt (see color plate).

This garden is the work of Mr. Sundar Shadi of India who, many years ago, specialized in the study of tropical horticulture at the University of California at Berkeley. For the past six years he has planted some 8000 annuals in Persian rug patterns which he has sketched during the winter months. Although the garden represents a hobby during his retirement years, it also is a gift to Mr. Shadi's community and thousands of visitors.

Each flowery Persian carpet is about twenty-eight by forty-five feet; the quilt is somewhat larger. Mr. Shadi delights in arranging strong color contrasts, easy to see from the sidewalk below, for this garden can be enjoyed by the public at any time—even from the windows of a car. There are deep blue lobelias, brilliant petunias, marigolds, verbenas, yellow violas, nemesias, nasturtiums—all flowers which bloom for months without interruption. The carpets become beautiful about mid-June, and are at their height of color on the 4th of July. They continue to be lovely into mid-August, but then the heavy fogs begin rolling in from the bay and gradually ruin the flowers. Making Persian rugs of flowers is very appropriate, for many such carpets are actually garden plans filled in with blossoms.

In the fall Mr. Shadi removes all the plants and starts getting ready for his Nativity scene, which is said to be the largest Christmas display of its kind in America. About 70,000 people from California and other states drive many miles to see his "Little Town of Bethlehem" (with some forty houses) and the remainder of the places and characters in the story, which cover the entire hillside.

For his 1976 project, he is planting his flowers in the design of the bicentennial flag. Also, as a gesture to the original inhabitants of our country, there will be an American Indian rug. These, however, will not eliminate his favorite plantings; there will also be three new and different Persian carpets.

ADDRESS: 944 Arlington Ave., El Cerrito, CA 94530. Telephone: 415-526-6658.

DIRECTIONS: El Cerrito is just north of Berkeley. Mr. Shadi's garden is so famous locally that anyone can give directions to his street.

Glendale

Friendship Garden

This Japanese Friendship Garden has an interesting story behind it. In 1960, Dr. Hideji Yamasaki, former mayor of Hiraoka, Japan, was in the United States. He was searching for a city which would closely resemble his own. The size and location of Glendale seemed to him to be ideal; therefore, he and Glendale Mayor Cal Cannon agreed on a sister city relationship. A special committee, together with the Chevy Chase Estates Garden Club, selected a site covering just over an acre, and raised funds to assist in creating the garden. In 1965 several cities in Japan were incorporated into Higashiosaka including Hiraoka, the result in California being a much longer name for the project: Glendale-Higashiosaka Sister City Program.

The garden was opened to the public in October 1974. It was designed by Eljiro Nunokawa, who had also drawn the plans for Descanso Gardens in La Canada. The teahouse has a charming name: *Sho-Shei-An,* meaning "Teahouse of the Whispering Pines." Near it is a stone purification basin, and throughout the garden one may see stone lanterns of the *yukimi, kasuga* and *oribe* types. The central feature is a pond, surrounded by trees of great variety, including flowering cherries, Japanese black pine, flowering pear, Japanese maple and Oriental magnolia.

OPEN: Daily, but *by appointment only,* from the Parks and Recreation Division, 613 E. Broadway, Room 120, Glendale, CA 91201. Telephone: 213-956-2000.

Teahouse in the Friendship Garden. (City of Glendale Parks & Recreation)

ADMISSION: Free.

ADDRESS: Friendship Garden, Brand Park, 1601 W. Mountain, Glendale, CA 91201.

MAINTAINED BY: The Glendale-Higashiosaka Sister City Committee, churches, cultural and business groups of Glendale, and residents of both Glendale and Higashiosaka, Japan.

La Canada

Descanso Gardens

Descanso Gardens are famous for their 100,000 camellias, the "History of Roses" garden, and other areas with flowers. They also include two Oriental gardens.

One is the Oriental teahouse with blue-tiled roof, where refreshments are served. In front of it is a small Japanese garden including a bright red bridge crossing a little stream.

The most unique garden here, however, is often not discovered by visitors, and has had little publicity. This is unfortunate, for the little Chinese Courtyard Garden behind Hospitality House on the hill is a real gem, in the true Chinese tradition. Although encompassing only about 560 square feet, it is full of charming authentic detail. Designed by Lawrence R. Moss, AILA, it was completed in the spring of 1970.

The enclosing white wall has an octagonal moon gate, through which one gets a first glimpse of the carefully planted garden. First, however, one should admire the eighteenth-century frieze of Chinese tiles on the outside wall. There are birds and flowers in high relief glazed in soft colors—violet blue, jade green and saffron yellow. Among them is a phoenix, symbol of immortality; cranes and waterfowl. Underneath are bright ceramic openwork windows.

There are similar tile panels inside the garden, dating from the end of the reign of Emperor Ch'ien Lung (1736-1795). The flowers in the design are all symbolic: the plum, peony, lotus and chrysanthemum standing for the Four Seasons; the peach, pomegranate and "Buddha's Hand" (citron) representing the Three Fruits; and years, sons and happiness representing the Three Abundances. The plum, pine and bamboo are the Three Friends, sometimes believed to be symbolic of China's great religions—Buddhism, Taoism and Confucianism. On the far side of the wall are two immortals—probably part of a frieze including all eight. Another tile shows a fierce Kylin with the head of a dragon, deer's hooves and a thrashing tail.

Looking through the moon gate, or when seated on the bench inside, the visitor can appreciate the little garden. This consists of a very small pond against the wall, surrounded by some well-chosen rocks, shrubs and ferns. The pool is fed from an antique brass lion's head spout. The atmosphere of rest and quiet beauty is perfect in this little Chinese courtyard garden.

OPEN: Daily, Mon. through Fri., 8 a.m. to 5:30 p.m.; Sat. and Sun., 8 a.m. to 6:30 p.m. Tram tours Tues. through Fri., 1-4 p.m.; Sat. and Sun., 10:30 a.m. to 4:30 p.m. (These go up the long hill to Hospitality House where one can get out and stay a while in the Chinese Garden.)

Below, a detail of the tiles on the wall of the Chinese garden at Descanso Gardens. Right, the Little Chinese Garden seen through the Moon Gate. (Photos by James L. McFadden)

Typical rock formations in the Chinese garden at Descanso Gardens. (Bill Abell)

ADMISSION: Free.

ADDRESS: Descanso Gardens, 1418 Descanso Dr., La Canada, CA 91011. Telephone: 213-790-5571, or 213-681-0331.

MAINTAINED BY: The County of Los Angeles, Department of Arboreta and Botanical Gardens.

DIRECTIONS: From Foothill Freeway (118) turn onto S-2 south, follow Descanso Gardens signs.

Lodi

Japanese Rock Garden

It is unusual to find a peaceful Japanese garden within a county recreational park that includes swimming pools and a zoo. But here it is, welcoming tired mothers, refreshing the elderly; a place of beauty appreciated by all ages.

The Japanese Rock Garden is a three-acre part of Micke Grove Park on 133 acres of land donated to San Joaquin County by philanthropist William G. Micke. It was created by the Japanese-American Citizens' League of nearby Stockton, and opened to the public in 1965. The garden was designed by Nagao Sakurai, retired head caretaker of the emperor's palace gardens in Tokyo, and the first graduated landscape architect from the Imperial University of Japan.

The garden surrounds a pond with some 200 *koi* (carp) which were the gift of the Japanese Agricultural Department. Two bridges, one bright red and one of dark natural wood, are decorative elements. Kofu City, Japan, donated a stone pagoda; and a beautiful *Kasuga*-type lantern, over 100 years old, was given by Shimizu City. Many other varieties of stone lanterns are scattered through the garden.

The place is especially lovely in spring when some sixty flowering Japanese cherries are in bloom, as well as plums, camellias and

The pond in Micke Grove Park. (Lodi District Chamber of Commerce)

azaleas. These are set against a background of black pines and other evergreens. Feathery bamboos and willows show lighter greens around the pond.

OPEN: From 8 a.m. to 7 p.m. daily, including all holidays except Christmas Day. Micke Grove Park has an interesting zoo, a children's playground, swimming pools and large picnic areas. Groups wishing to reserve picnic space or the open-air dance floor should telephone 209-369-2205 in Lodi; or 209-948-1383 in Stockton.

ADMISSION: Free.

ADDRESS: Micke Grove Park and Zoo, Micke Grove Rd., Lodi, CA 95240.

Los Angeles

UCLA Japanese Garden

Here is an authentic Japanese hill-and-pond garden laid out on a steep hillside, with many fascinating decorative features. It was once part of the estate of Mr. and Mrs. Gordon Guiberson, who created it as a memorial to Mr. Guiberson's mother. In 1965 it was donated to the University of California at Los Angeles by Mr. Edward W. Carter, then chairman of the regents of the university. Today it is used as an adjunct to the teaching programs of several UCLA departments including biology, art and architecture.

In order to create a perfect example of Japanese garden art, Mr. and Mrs. Guiberson traveled thousands of miles. They personally selected many of the stones, basins, bridges and artifacts to be found here, and devoted long months to the plans. The original design was by Nagao Sakurai. A few years after it was completed, however, very heavy rains caused much of this ravine garden to collapse, and Professor Koichi Kawana of UCLA was brought in to reconstruct and redesign it.

It is a very beautiful garden with many unusual characteristics. Its main entrance gate is similar to that of the famous Ichida estate in Kyoto. Made for the California garden first in Kyoto, with

Above, entrance gate to the U.C.L.A. Japanese garden. Below, small waterfall, rocks, and lantern. (Photos by James L. McFadden)

tongue-and-groove construction, using pegs instead of nails, it was then taken apart, shipped to America and rebuilt here under the supervision of its designer. At the base of the entry walls lie black slate rocks found only in the mountains near Nara, Japan. The bamboo fence beyond the gateway walls is copied from the fences at the Katsura Detached Palace in Kyoto.

The selection and careful placement of the many rocks in this garden make them one of its main attractions. Some 400 tons of lichen-covered, dark brown stones came from Santa Paula Canyons; several hundred tons of slightly lighter rocks were brought from quarries at the foot of Mt. San Antonio northeast of Los Angeles; while special ornamental specimens were selected by the Guibersons in Kyoto, Osaka, and Tokyo, Japan. Along the path not far from the entrance there are two especially interesting carved stones: one representing the goddess Kuan Yin in low relief; the other, a 1000-year-old treasure, is ornamented with figures of Buddha seated in sixteen positions. Among the several kinds of stone purification basins, one of the most beautiful is a cube called "Buddha Facing Four Directions" (see color plate). This type originated in Kamakura around 1300 A.D., and was also used occasionally as a pagoda base.

Another stone receives water dripping from a bamboo pipe, which falls regularly as it becomes full, making a clanking sound. In Japan these were used as "wild boar scarers," but here they serve to frighten raccoons who might try to eat the beautiful carp in the pool! The stone paths are of a variety of types: some are patterned similarly to the *tatami* mats used in Japanese houses; another, beside the pond, is made of old mill stones; while some concrete walks have random patterns of inset polished black stone. The flooring of the "moon-viewing platform" and shrine deck is made of stones set in the "butterfly pattern" by Mr. K. Nakamura. He also decorated the front of the barbecue counter (now used to display bonsai trees in bowls) with a design representing chrysanthemums and camellias.

The small pond at the base of the hill is fed from a little waterfall. A large flat stone at its edge is the traditional Japanese "thinking stone" where the owner could kneel and contemplate the water or his garden. In the pond itself lies a "turtle stone" representing long life, and nearby is a large "noble ship stone" symbolic of a ship at sea—both originally from Kyoto.

The fat little Korean lantern at water's edge represents a lighthouse, with a black pebble beach below. Two large rectangular rocks near the millstone path are called "devil casting stones," as a person walking on them could suddenly step aside and let a pursuing devil fall into the water. Blue water lilies and lotus decorate the pond as do the colorful *koi* (carp).

A five-story stone pagoda makes a tall accent below the pond. Beyond, the steep path leads up on the left to a large garden house for rest, contemplation, and the tea ceremony. Some of the articles used for the latter are placed on view here. Still higher up, on the other side of the garden, there is a lovely small Hokora Shrine (see color plate) containing an old, rare Buddha of gilded wood. This shrine was made by the same Kyoto artisans who constructed the entrance gate. The roof is of Japanese cryptomeria. The bronze ornamental door fixtures were smoked by burning cedar leaves. Custom-made bronze lamps hang from the roof. Two stone Chinese lion-dogs guard the entrance. Below this, on the moon-viewing platform, is a potted wisteria 120 years old.

When the quantities of azaleas are in bloom up the slopes of the ravine, this is a spectacular, colorful garden. At other seasons it presents a quieter scene, accented here and there with red or golden yellow cut-leaf maples.

OPEN: Open only by appointment. Due to the fact that there is no parking space, and parking along the street on either side is forbidden, admission to the garden is possible *only* by making an advance appointment by telephone (213-825-4574). Very small groups of students of landscape architecture or with other valid special interests are then taken by staff from the UCLA Botanical Gardens on Tuesdays between 10 a.m. and 1 p.m., or Wednesdays from noon to 3 p.m.

Los Angeles (Hollywood)

Yamashiro Restaurant

This replica of a mountain palace in Japan was built over sixty years ago by two importers of antiques to house their fabulous

Oriental treasures. It was named for the province which surrounds that jewel of Japanese garden art, Kyoto. Yamashiro means "mountain palace," and this unique Oriental structure with its fascinating authentic details is indeed palatial, a Japanese vision high up on a hill overlooking the lights and skyscrapers of modern Hollywood.

Unfortunately the building and grounds underwent drastic

The old Japanese black pines. (James L. McFadden)

changes during World War II and the years following—being transformed into a military school, the entire structure painted black, the twelve acres of gardens destroyed. Since 1960 the present owners have undertaken the herculean task of gradually restoring the house, grounds and ornamental structures to their former beauty.

The original three terraces below the building are still intact. The first one on the steep descent, originally ornamented with tiny Japanese houses, pagodas and bridges as a miniature Japan, is now a restful garden. The sixty-year-old Japanese black pines, bent and twisted into beautiful artistic shapes, are perhaps the oldest of their kind in America. Richard Ota, Japanese landscape architect and vice-president of the Southern California Bonsai Society, watches over them as if they were his favorite children. He spends hours twice a year hand-plucking the newly sprouted "candles" on the branches to stunt their growth and keep each tree form in perfect proportion. A small irregular pool and some well-chosen rocks complete the picture. The terrace just below is planted with velvety Korean grass, and is an exquisite picture in slanting late afternoon sunlight when each little hump of green casts its own shadow.

An old Japanese gate with fine black and white ornamentation marks the center of the third terrace. Paths on each side lead downward to an imported red and black *torii* gate, the entrance to the modern swimming pool. Yet even in this American recreational environment one has only to look up to see a splendid 600-year-old Japanese pagoda towering above a rocky bit of Oriental garden. It will not be long before this Japanese palace and its gardens will be completely authentic, offering guests a visit to the Land of the Rising Sun. Even now, enjoying wonderful meals and drinks on the open verandas or in the garden courtyard within the building, one has many reminders of being in a delightful Japanese environment.

OPEN: Daily and in the evenings.

ADDRESS: 1999 North Sycamore Ave., Hollywood, CA 90068. Telephone: 213-466-5125.

DIRECTIONS: Take the Hollywood Freeway to the Highland

offramp. Take Highland to Franklin (one long block north of Hollywood Blvd.). Go west on Franklin to Sycamore. Turn right (north) on Sycamore, winding up the hill to the right, following the Yamashiro signs.

Japanese gate in garden at Yamashiro Restaurant. (James L. McFadden)

Los Angeles (Hollywood)

Japanese Garden in Wattles Gardens Park

This charming little Japanese garden dates back to the early twentieth century. It is one of the few former private estate gardens of that period now open to the public.

When Mr. Gurdon W. Wattles, an Omaha banker, railroad financier and civic leader, decided to build a summer home in Hollywood, he bought a large tract of land, laying out some fifty acres of it in gardens. One of these gardens was inspired by the arts and gardens of Japan which particularly impressed Mr. and Mrs. Wattles during a trip around the world.

They engaged landscape architect Fugio of Japan as designer. All the decorative objects as well as the shrubs and plants came to America by ship—stone lanterns, pagodas, a Shinto shrine, a *torii* gate and two stone lions among them. For many happy years as many as 100 guests at a time enjoyed garden parties here, strolling in the rose garden and other areas as well, in the light of many paper Japanese lanterns. On one day a week the grounds were also open to the general public.

As the years went by, however, things changed. Vandals took a great toll. The Recreation and Parks Department was able to purchase the land for a park, but lack of money continued to be a problem for upkeep. Professor Koichi Kawana, well-known landscape architect of Los Angeles, was asked to redesign the Japanese garden in the park, but much of his plan still remains uncompleted.

The large lantern at the street entrance was the gift of Japan Airlines in commemoration of ten years of service between Los Angeles and Japan. The teahouse nearby was donated by the *Omote-senke* of Japan, one of the three great tea ceremony organizations. Going on up the steep hill one comes to another fine stone lantern at the actual garden gate. This was a gift in 1963 from Los Angeles' Sister City of Nagoya. Beyond the roofed gate lies a little pool fed by a small waterfall. Winding paths lead around and up the rocky hillside to the Shinto shrine. This is a quiet, remote place, seemingly miles away from the bustle on the streets of Hollywood.

Entrance gate in Wattles Gardens. (James L. McFadden)

OPEN: Daily from 10 a.m. to 4 p.m.

ADMISSION: Free.

ADDRESS: 1824 North Curson Ave., Hollywood, CA 90028.

DIRECTIONS: From Hollywood Blvd. go north on Curson Ave. to the gate on the right.

Monterey Park

Nachi Gardens

This is a new little park, still being developed by the local Japanese community. There is a *torii* gate at the entrance, a stone purification basin, and an *azumaia* (resting shelter) with picnic tables in it. The stone Japanese lantern has been broken off by vandals—a problem which, unfortunately, is well known in our public gardens today. The garden is being carefully planted.

Nachi Gardens are sponsored by the Sister City Association of Monterey Park, in honor of Nachikatsuura in Japan, and was dedicated in December 1970.

The gardens are located within Sequoia Park, a large recreational area on Ridge Crest Street, which is lined with very lovely homes, each having neat, authentic Japanese landscaping.

ADDRESS: Nachi Gardens, Ridge Crest St., Monterey Park. Mail: Sister City Association, P.O. Box 482, Monterey Park, CA 91754.

DIRECTIONS: From Monterey Pass Rd. (near the firehouse) take Vagabond Rd. up the hill, then turn left onto Ridge Crest St.

Oakland

Japanese Garden at Oakland-East Bay Garden Center, Inc.

This Japanese garden is an excellent example of authentic design and interesting detail applied to a small area—in this case, a plot fifty by seventy-five feet. The effect is one of space, tranquility and great beauty.

It was created in 1959 through the combined efforts and contributions of the Japanese-American community, garden clubs, plant societies, the city parks department, and a long list of generous merchants and nurserymen. Hisaichi Harry Tsugawa designed and supervised the entire construction and planting.

Included in the plan is an irregular pool with a curved bridge of gray stone, and a bamboo *azumaia* (a resting place). At intervals one sees a number of Japanese lanterns and a stone purification basin; but the main interest perhaps lies in the delightful symbolism of the carefully selected stones. There are seventeen of these, singly or in groups, with Japanese names denoting "three wise men"; "rock wants to be by himself"; "fish swimming"; "moon shadow rock"; "tiger lookout rock"; and three rocks as a family of father, mother and child. An island in the pool is called "live long time island," symbolizing great gentleness, longevity and happiness

(Photos of Lakeside Park Garden Center by Kaz Tsuruta)

for those who own the garden. Among the plantings one sees maples, pines, bamboo and various grasses; a few azaleas; and iris and water lilies in the pool. Truly a garden for thoughtful meditation and relaxation!

OPEN: From 10 a.m. to 4 p.m. daily.

ADMISSION: Free.

ADMINISTERED BY: The City of Oakland Parks and Recreation Department, 1520 Lakeside Dr., Oakland, CA 94602. Telephone: 415-273-3062.

ADDRESS: Oakland-East Bay Garden Center, Inc., 666 Bellevue Ave., Oakland, CA 94602. Mail: P.O. Box 2774, Oakland, CA 94602.

Oroville

Chinese Temple Garden

The Chinese Temple at Oroville is now over 100 years old and has been designated a State Historical Landmark. It is unique in America, and its splendid restoration and preservation are a tribute to the citizens of this old gold-mining town. The courtyard garden, which was added to the complex in 1968, is authentically Chinese both in its structure and its plantings. The plans were donated by architect Philip Choy, while the landscaping was designed and supervised by Mrs. Cabot (Margaret) Brown, planting consultant to Golden Gate Park in San Francisco.

The brick flooring of the courtyard is laid out in interesting patterns, with hexagonal openings here and there for small trees.

Chinese Temple courtyard. (Oroville Park Commission)

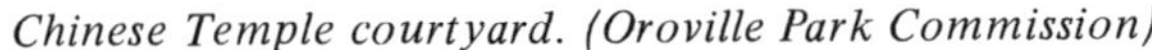

These are all of Chinese origin and symbolism: the pine signifying hardiness, strength of character, as well as silence and solitude; the plum, beloved harbinger of spring; the peach standing for long life and protection from demons; the bamboo for lasting friendship and hardy old age. There are a number of tallow trees, which were used in China to make candle wicks; and the Pomolo grapefruit, which ripens at the time of the Chinese New Year. Around the temple other trees of Chinese origin have also been planted: the ginkgo, persimmon, pistachio, loquat, Chinese flame tree and dawn redwood. Among the flowers are peonies, chrysanthemums, *Rosa hugonis, Narcissus tazetta* (Chinese lily), Oriental poppies, and many others. There is a large rock of Butte County jade, and a jade tree.

The patterns decorating the top of the surrounding fence, the openwork wall, the large roofed gate, the copper pavilion roof donated by the Chan family—all are true to the traditions of the old Chinese courtyard gardens, making this one, too, a place of tranquil beauty.

The history of this Chinese Temple is a fascinating one. There was a large colony of Chinese working in the gold mines of Bidwell Bar, which began to dwindle in the 1850s due to floods and diminishing returns of gold. The Chinese then moved to what is now the town of Oroville and, in about 1870, erected a temple of worship there. By the time of the depression in the 1920s, however, the Chinese population had decreased, and the building and its contents fell into disrepair, a prey to the weather, fire and vandals. Members of the Chan family, original settlers, continued to pay the taxes, but it was only in 1937 that the remaining Chinese residents consented to turning the property over to the city council and park commission.

In 1940, due especially to the enthusiasm and interest of Mrs. Walter W. Reece, the Oroville Women's Community Club made the restoration of the Chinese Temple its special project. Contributions began to come in from all sides: some in cash, others in unpaid work at the buildings. The labor unions offered their services free, the Rotary Club constructed the courtyard pergolas, and everyone pitched in. In 1968, a new Tapestry Hall was added to contain the priceless royal parasols, banners, costumes, jewelry,

etc., many being gifts from the Chinese emperor at the time of the temple's erection.

Today there are six parts to this historical complex: the Main Temple for Taoist worship; the Moon Temple (entered through a "moon gate") for the worship of Buddha; the Council Room in which the more learned Chinese advised the gold miners who were often illiterate; the Tapestry Hall with its large collection of Chinese art from Canton province; the Display Hall for recent gifts of Chinese artifacts; and the Chan Room, an ancestral worship chapel built in 1874, dedicated to the Chan family clan.

OPEN: Daily 10 a.m. to 4:30 p.m., except Wed. and Thurs. when the hours are noon to 4:30 p.m.

ADMISSION: Adults $1.00, children under 12 free with an adult. The ticket also includes admission to the nearby Victorian Lott House. Brochure about temple, 75¢.

ADDRESS: 1500 Broderick St., behind the Feather River Levee. For information phone 916-533-1496, or Chamber of Commerce, 916-533-2542.

MAINTAINED BY: Oroville Park Department.

DIRECTIONS: Oroville is 75 miles northeast of Sacramento. From State Highway 70, exit at Montgomery St. and drive east; the green stripe painted on the road leads to the temple.

Pacific Palisades

Self-Realization Fellowship Lake Shrine

This Lake Shrine of the Self-Realization Fellowship is not really an Oriental garden in the traditional sense. But we felt it should be included in this book because it is a place designed for quiet meditation around a beautiful small lake, with some interesting Oriental features.

Even on a Sunday afternoon when we were there with many others, no running and screaming of children and no loud talking disturbed the peaceful atmosphere. Everyone seemed happy just

Reflection pool around the courtyard of the Chinese Temple in Oroville. (Byron Boots)

to walk around the edge of the water among the ten acres of luxurious, natural California shrubs and trees—truly a place of serenity.

A great carved stone sarcophagus from China, said to be 1000 years old, holds some of the ashes of Mahatma Gandhi. It is flanked by two statues of Kuan Yin, Goddess of Mercy. The plaque in front of it reads: "Mahatma Gandhi World Peace Memorial, Dedicated to World Brotherhood, August 20, 1950, by Paramahansa Yogananda and Lt. Gov. Goodwin Knight." One of

(Photos by James L. McFadden)

Gandhi's statements defines the spirit of this Lake Shrine: "Life is an aspiration. Its mission is to strive after perfection, which is self-realization. The ideal must not be lowered because of our weaknesses or imperfections."

Between this sarcophagus and the lake is a large "Golden Lotus Archway" symbolizing divine unfoldment. It is a structure truly reminiscent of India, and especially lovely when seen with its reflection from across the lake. The small island at one end of the lake is a refuge for ducks, mud hens, and swans from South

America and Holland. Of special horticultural and historic interest is the "bo" tree near the Lotus Archway. It is unique in America as the only authentic "descendant" of the highly venerated "bo" or "Bodhi" tree in Gaya, India, under which Buddha sat in meditation and attained spiritual illumination. A cutting from the original tree was sent to Ceylon in the third century B.C. by King Asoka, and it flourished there for 2300 years. From this, a cutting was made in 1954 by the Burmese ambassador to Ceylon, and presented to the Rev. Leslie Lowe, president of the Universal Buddhist Fellowship, who gave it to the Self-Realization Fellowship grounds in 1957.

Services in the small chapel are attended by people from every faith. This Lake Shrine is only one of the many centers for retreat and study founded by Paramahansa Yogananda all over the United States and in India.

OPEN: Daily 10 a.m. to 5 p.m., except Mondays.

ADMISSION: Free.

ADDRESS: 17190 Sunset Blvd., Pacific Palisades, CA 90272. Telephone: 213-225-1811.

San Diego (Mission Bay)

Japanese Village at Sea World

The Japanese Village at Sea World, an eighty-acre park with dramatic marine shows, has been skillfully landscaped in the Japanese tradition by Tokyo's famous landscape architect, Dr. Kubo. It covers some two acres, with authentic plantings and a wandering stream with waterfalls and a pool abounding in wild fowl and *koi* (carp). This area is a restful oasis in the park even when there are crowds of visitors.

The large, two-story teahouse where refreshments are served was copied from Kyoto's Golden Pavilion. On its balconies visitors relax and enjoy the surrounding beauty. There are interesting stone lanterns, a dove pavilion where children may feed the birds, and a number of stone pagodas. Near the salt water pool where

A rough stone lantern and water fowl. (James L. McFadden)

Japanese girl divers plunge in to retrieve oysters for pearls, there is a temple bell to honor the souls of the departed oysters.

Like all the rest of Sea World's beautifully landscaped grounds, the Japanese Village is constantly groomed to keep it neat and in good condition. It is an excellent example of how a commercial enterprise can attain an atmosphere of restful good taste and a carefully planned flow for the thousands who visit it, without any sense of overcrowding.

OPEN: Daily throughout the year from 9:30 a.m. to dusk.

ADMISSION TO SEA WORLD: Adults, $5.00; children 4 to 12, $2.75; under 4, free.

Sea World's Japanese Village. Above, teahouse; below, "Spirit Shrine." (Photos by James L. McFadden)

ADDRESS OF GARDEN: 1720 South Shores Dr., Mission Bay, San Diego, CA 92109. Public relations office: Telephone: 714-222-6363.

DIRECTIONS: Follow Sea World signs from Rte. I-5.

San Diego

Proposed Japanese Garden for Balboa Park

This project, to which 4½ acres in Balboa Park have been allocated, will be a new Japanese garden to be located in the canyon behind the ancient Japanese gate just north of the Organ Pavilion. The gate was a gift to the city of San Diego from the San Diego-Yokohama Sister City Society. It is said to be over a century old, perhaps predating the opening of the port of Yokohama to world commerce. It was dedicated to a former mayor, the late Charles C. Dail, who was instrumental in forming the Sister City organization in 1956.

At that time the city of Yokohama gave a beautiful stone snow-viewing lantern to the society, which was placed in the Zoological Gardens of Balboa Park. In return, the society sent a replica of Donal Hord's famous "Guardian of the Waters" statue to Yokohama, where it now stands in Yamashita Park.

The new Japanese garden will be of the hill-and-pond stroll garden type. Paths will lead down along waterfalls, a pond, and a pavilion for serving tea. The San Diego-Yokohama Sister City Society is hopeful that enough donations from the public will assist the city in making this dream of a Japanese garden come true. It would be a splendid addition to this historic and beautiful park, which dates back to 1868, and was the site of the Panama-California International Exposition in 1910, and the California-Pacific International Exposition of 1935-36.

OPEN: Balboa Park is open daily.

ADMISSION: Free.

ADDRESS: The San Diego-Yokohama Sister City Society, Studio

\# 2, House of Hospitality, Balboa Park, San Diego. Mail: P.O. Box 2842, San Diego, CA 92112.

DIRECTIONS: To reach Balboa Park, follow signs along highways. Turn off Rte. I-5 onto Laurel, follow this to the end.

The ancient Japanese gateway, which will become the entrance to the proposed new Japanese garden. (James L. McFadden)

San Francisco

Japanese Tea Garden in Golden Gate Park

The Japanese Tea Garden in Golden Gate Park, the oldest Japanese garden still open to the American public today, is an historic landmark. When the California Midwinter Exposition was being planned in an effort to counteract the financial depression of 1893, a Japanese village was included as one feature. It was the brainchild of George Turner Marsh, an Australian who had lived in Japan for five years. Fascinated by Japan's art, he had opened America's first Oriental art goods store in San Francisco, an establishment which is still owned by his descendants. The original Japanese village at the Exposition of 1894 is today the three-acre Tea Garden.

Mr. Marsh imported both the materials and the workmen from Japan, and, in fluent Japanese, directed the construction himself. He was enthusiastically assisted by the Scotsman John McLaren, who was to serve as San Francisco's park superintendent for fifty-six years. Many of the plantings which we see in this garden today were the work of Makoto Hagiwara. These include the cherry trees remaining from the 3,000 trees which he originally planted. He was in charge of the garden for many years and, upon his death in 1925, his family continued his work. The Japanese government rewarded Hagiwara's efforts by making him a baron. America, however, during World War II, relocated the Hagiwara family in a concentration camp, and their home in the Tea Garden was torn down.

The splendid two-story gate which is now the garden entrance had been built originally for Mr. Marsh's own Japanese garden by his head carpenter, Nakatani, but was moved to become part of the Exposition's Japanese complex. It contains hundreds of pieces of hand-carved wood. The large white stone lantern across the pool from the penance steps is another of the original ornaments. The penance steps were deliberately made very steep to encourage meditation along the climb to the large *torii*, which frames the tall pink pagoda. The pagoda, a Buddhist shrine of five stories built to contain scriptures, came from the Panama-Pacific Exposition of 1916 in San Diego as a later addition to this garden. The nine rings

on the spire represent the various heavens of the gods. The highly arched drum bridge of dark wood is another traditional Japanese device used in front of shrines to induce a reverent attitude and test a person's religious zeal.

A beautiful bronze peace lantern was presented to the garden in 1953 by the Mothers' Association of the Japanese Kindergarten League. It was bought with money contributed by thousands of children in Japan. Near the teahouse, where refreshments are served by pretty Japanese girls, there is a large stone boat-shaped purification basin from a villa in Tokyo. The water flowing from this basin runs into a small stream winding through the garden. The great bronze Buddha nearby broods in the shade of tall trees. Weighing 1½ tons, it was cast in 1790 in Tajima Province, Honshu, for the Taionji Temple. Donated by the S. and G. Gump Company, it is called the *Amazarashi-No-Hotoke*, "The Buddha that sits throughout the sunny and rainy weather without a shelter."

In 1953 the new Classical Garden was presented to San Francisco by Japan. It was designed by the famous landscape architect Nagao Sakurai. This is a modernized version of Japanese landscaping in the Muromachi Period of about 500 years ago. Two upright stones represent a waterfall; bushes in the background give the effect of hills and mountains. White sand with raked "wave" lines symbolize the water surrounding small rock "islands." In 1960 Mr. Sakurai also redesigned much of the front pool area and the grounds around the teahouse. In 1965 a spendid collection of plants, bonsai trees, lanterns and stones willed to the garden by Dr. and Mrs. Hugh Frazer led to a major redevelopment of the western section of the garden, which included a fine waterfall. Immediately following the redevelopment, the Brundage Oriental Wing of the de Young Museum next door was completed. In order to make a more restful scene as observed from the new picture windows of the museum, Roy L. Hudson redesigned a part of the garden.

It would be impossible in this brief outline of the history of the Tea Garden to mention all of the beautiful features contributed by donors. There is a danger, however (which the Park Department is undoubtedly aware of) that too many additional gifts and memorial plaques will clutter up the original peaceful design. The brilliant red structures make the Tea Garden a spectacular tourist

The pink pagoda. (James L. McFadden)

Golden Gate Park. Above, one of the gates to the Japanese Tea Garden; below, the steep wooden drum bridge. (Photos by James L. McFadden)

attraction. One of its main assets, however, is the excellent variety of colors and textures in the original plantings of evergreens. To appreciate these, one should take the time to wander quietly through the garden in the early morning hours before the busloads of sightseers arrive (see color plate).

OPEN: Daily, 8 a.m. to dusk.

ADMISSION: Free.

MAINTAINED BY: The San Francisco Recreation and Park Department, Fell and Stanton Sts., San Francisco, CA 94117.

San Francisco

Moon-Viewing Pavilion Garden in Strybing Arboretum

The Moon-Viewing Pavilion Garden is a fairly recent addition to the famous plantings in Strybing Arboretum in Golden Gate Park. It was presented to the community in 1973 as a gift from the San Francisco Bay Area Chapter of Ikebana International. To raise the needed funds for this lovely Japanese garden, this dedicated organization worked hard for five years, gathering donations and proceeds from flower shows. Designed by Henry Matsutani, this 1½ acre garden is intended to represent a small portion of the famous Katsura Imperial Gardens in Kyoto, created in the early seventeenth century. As in its prototype, an irregularly shaped pond is the central feature, fed by a rivulet which is flanked by twenty-five varieties of Japanese iris. A small island in the pond represents a turtle, symbol of long life.

The central point of interest is the Moon-Viewing Pavilion, a platform jutting out over the water. In Japan, parties were held on nights of the full moon. The royal guests would compose verses while seated on cushions enjoying the moonlight and its reflections in the water. The moon is always associated with Katsura because that name is also the word for a certain tree (*Cercidiphyllum japonicum*) which, according to legend, grows on the moon. Opposite the platform in the arboretum's garden there is a stone lantern on a peninsula, symbolizing a landing place where boats may be guided by its light.

The platform for moon viewing in Strybing Arboretum. (Kaz Tsuruta)

This is a beautiful, restful Japanese stroll garden, its rocks and plants carefully chosen and placed. To achieve a moss garden effect, *Hernaria glabra* was used as more suited to the San Francisco climate, and plants were selected to give pleasure throughout the year. An *akebobo* (flowering cherry) and the rare rhododendron "Autumn Gold" are delightful features planted as memorials.

This garden is only a small part of the interesting Strybing Arboretum which encompasses seventy-five acres. There are outstanding collections of trees from around the world; the Garden of Fragrance for the blind; the Shakespeare Garden; the Redwood Trail; the Succulent Garden; the John Muir Nature Trail; the conservatory; and the series of Sunset Demonstration Gardens planned for home gardeners of this area.

OPEN: Weekdays 8 a.m. to 4:30 p.m.; Sat., Sun. and holidays 10 a.m. to 5 p.m. Guided tours available.

ADMISSION: Free.

ADDRESS: Strybing Arboretum, between 9th and 15th Avenues adjacent to Lincoln Way, in Golden Gate Park. Mail address: Strybing Arboretum Society of Golden Gate Park, 9th Ave. at Lincoln Way, San Francisco, CA 94122. Telephone: 415-661-0822.

MAINTAINED BY: The Strybing Arboretum Society and the San Francisco Recreation and Park Department.

San Jose

Japanese Friendship Garden

This delightful Japanese Friendship Garden was a result of San Jose's relationship with her Sister City, Okayama, Japan, and was patterned after Okayama's Korakuen Garden. It was dedicated in 1965.

The zigzag bridge and pool in the Japanese Friendship Garden. (Charles M. Hayes)

It is quite a large "stroll garden," with paths winding around two ponds. In the small lower pond, an island is named for its shape, the "Turtle Island." Some 3000 *koi* (carp) were flown over from Japan in 1966 for the ponds. One tall granite lantern is 400 years old; and another large lantern weighing three tons was donated by the city of Okayama. There are two bridges of different types: one is the high curved "drum" bridge; the other a zigzag plank bridge designed to keep evil spirits from following, as they were said to be able to go only in straight lines. A small waterfall connects the two ponds. In a grassy area a large rock next to a smaller one denotes the "father and son" rocks; a group beyond is called "the three wise men"; while a single tall rock is a "soldier stone" or "guardian rock." The cherry trees along the fence near the main gate are another lovely reminder of Japan in the spring. Nearby is a teahouse where refreshments are served.

OPEN: Daily, dawn to dusk. The teahouse and gift shop are open from 11 a.m. to 5 p.m. daily except Mondays.

ADMISSION: Free.

ADDRESS: 1490 Senter Rd., San Jose, CA 95100. For groups wishing meals served at the teahouse, telephone 408-294-4706. The Japanese Friendship Garden is part of Kelley Park.

San Jose

Japanese Garden at the Buddhist Temple

This small but very authentic Buddhist temple was designed by Shizaburo Nishiura, who also planned the Hakone Gardens in Saratoga. The Japanese garden at one side (about 50' x 125') is a lovely quiet spot. Its irregularly shaped pond, filled with bright colored *koi* (carp), is surrounded by very fine evergreens. A stone bridge crosses the water, and a *Kasuga* lantern is a prominent feature. The garden was designed by Mr. Earnest Uenaka almost twenty years ago.

The temple is well known in this part of California for its celebration of the Obon Festival in July. These traditional events date back more than a thousand years. They originated in Japan around 500 A.D. to rejoice at the end of the season of heavy monsoons, when the monks had been kept indoors, unable to go about their missions. Today, Buddhist temples all over America have Obon Festivals with dancing in the streets under blazing lanterns, and a gay country fair atmosphere. Most people who attend wear Japanese costumes, but anyone is welcome to join.

OPEN: The garden is open daily.

ADMISSION: Free.

ADDRESS: 640 North 5th St., San Jose, CA 95100. Temple telephone: 408-293-9292.

Japanese garden at the Buddhist Temple. (Charles M. Hayes)

San Marino

Japanese Garden
Huntington Library, Art Gallery & Botanical Gardens

The Japanese Garden is located in a canyon, beautifully land-scaped into a hill-and-pond stroll garden. Designed originally by William Hertrich, curator of the gardens for the estate of Henry Edwards Huntington, it was opened to the public in 1929. There is so much to see in these five acres that it is helpful to purchase the little guide pamphlet at the entrance (cost 10¢) in order to better understand the many Japanese features.

On each side of the entrance are Chinese lion-dogs as friendly guardians: the male dog on the left was supposed to guard the family's health; the female on the right, its spiritual life. There are a number of votive stones along the paths with carvings depicting Buddhist gods backed by a pointed "luminous cloud." The large bronze bell hanging in the tower near the gate was cast in 1766 for Kongo Buji Temple on Mt. Koya, a sacred mountain of Japan. Its striker is made of the flower stem of an agave plant.

The center of interest is the vermillion arched bridge over part of the lake in the basin of the canyon, its shape reflecting in the water like a full moon (see color plate). There are two statues of Buddha, and a variety of stone and metal lanterns and stone pagodas throughout the garden. On the far side is an interesting five-room Japanese house, part of which was brought from Japan. Visitors may not enter, but can see the rooms and their traditional furnishings through the open sides. Above this is the Ikebana House for classes and displays of flower arrangements. Adjoining this house and in the Bonsai Court are examples of *Sui-Seki*, water-sculptured stones chosen to represent some natural phenomenon—a mountain, a cascade, or an island—stimulating the imagination of the beholder.

A dry sand-and-stone Zen Garden, opened in 1968, has carefully selected rocks and raked sand backed by trees and shrubs, with a square-cut shrub providing a striking contrast. The col-

Entrance to Japanese garden at Huntington Botanical Gardens. (Huntington Library, Art Gallery & Botanical Gardens)

(Photo upper right, James L. McFadden. Photos upper left and below, courtesy Huntington Library, Art Gallery & Botanical Gardens)

lection of dwarfed trees in the Bonsai Court is well labeled to show many different types of this art form. The stone sculpture of a Buddhist priest in an attitude of prayer, found in this court, dates from the Edo period (seventeenth to mid-nineteenth century). The trees and shrubs throughout the garden have been carefully selected, mostly of Asiatic origin, with lovely wisteria and camellias adding seasonal color.

Visitors to this Japanese Garden will also want to spend time strolling through the famous Desert Garden with the largest collection of cacti and succulents in the world, a place of fantastic color and form; and the Rose Garden, Shakespeare Garden, Herb Garden, and Camellia Test Garden. The gardens are also the setting for many musical and dramatic entertainments.

OPEN: Tues. through Sun. 1-4:30 p.m. Closed Mondays and on major holidays, also during Oct.

ADMISSION: Free.

ADDRESS: Huntington Library, Art Gallery & Botanical Gardens, 1151 Oxford Rd., San Marino, CA 91108. Telephone: 213-792-6141, or 213-792-6601.

DIRECTIONS: San Marino is 5 miles west of Arcadia. From San Marino Blvd. northbound, go left on Oxford Rd. and follow signs.

San Mateo

Japanese Garden in Central Park

This Japanese Garden is a splendid example of community cooperation and enthusiasm. In 1963, San Mateo had formed a Sister City relationship with Toyanaka, Japan. The local Landscape Gardener's Association had already been considering creating a public Japanese garden. Soon members of this group and the Japanese-American community, garden clubs, civic associations and individuals began working together with the City Council and the Park and Recreation Department by donating time, money, plants, and even volunteer labor in order that this Japanese garden dream might come true. The garden was designed by Nagao

Sakurai, former landscape architect at the Imperial Palace in Tokyo. In two years, by 1965, the two-acre garden was formally opened to the public with a Shinto ceremony.

Near the dark wooden-roofed entrance gate there is an attractive teahouse tended by Japanese hostesses in bright kimonos.

The large irregularly shaped pond is fed by a rushing waterfall. Beside this stands a twelve-foot-high stone pagoda donated by Toyanaka, the Sister City. Up here there is also an *azumaya*, a viewing house, from which one can see the entire garden, the pond, occasional stone lanterns, and fine plantings among carefully placed rocks. The entire place has a feeling of spaciousness, of restraint and quiet beauty.

Side of the guest house in the Japanese garden. (James L. McFadden)

Above, hostess Dora Chuji Oiwa greets visitors to the Japanese garden; below, the teahouse. (Photos by James L. McFadden)

OPEN: Mon. through Fri., 8 a.m. to 4 p.m.; Sat. and Sun., 11 a.m. to 5 p.m. The teahouse is open with hostess from 11 a.m. to 4 p.m. in summer.

ADMISSION: Free.

ADDRESS: Japanese Garden in Central Park, at El Camino Rd. and 5th Ave., San Mateo, CA 94402.

MAINTAINED BY: The City Park and Recreation Department (telephone: 415-574-6730); aided financially by the Japanese-American community.

DIRECTIONS: From Bayshore Freeway (101) take San Mateo Third Ave. Exit west to El Camino Real; turn left on this to 5th Ave.

Saratoga

Hakone Gardens

The beautiful Hakone Gardens were completed in 1918 for the estate of Mrs. Oliver Charles Stine. She had spent six months in Japan and became enchanted with the traditional gardens there. She named her garden "Hakone" because it lies in the Congress Springs area which she felt resembled Fuji Hakone National Park in Japan. The garden was designed by Mr. N. Aihara, the son of the head gardener at the Imperial Palace in Tokyo. In 1941 the "mon" or main gate was created by Shinzaburo Nishiura. It is carefully put together of redwood and imported bamboo in the style of Kamakura temple architecture, and is flanked by two woven fences of contrasting design. There is a small Japanese teahouse nearby. In 1966 Hakone Gardens became a two-acre city park.

The moon-viewing house up on the hill, constructed in traditional style without the use of nails, was originally part of the Japanese exhibit at the 1915 San Francisco Exposition. From this building there is an excellent view of the pond with its tall threadlike fountain, natural wood bridges, and the fine old trees. Nearby is the three-step waterfall (symbol of earth, man and heaven), and a seventeenth-century image of Jizo Bosatsu, the

Hakone Gardens with its natural wood bridge and threadlike fountain. (James L. McFadden)

Buddhist patron saint of children and dead souls.

Walking around the pond, which is shaped like the Chinese character for "heart," one can see the many *koi* (carp), the water lilies, and the *ohga*, the beautiful "rose lotus" of the Far East. The path proceeds under a pergola draped with a very old wisteria vine. On the island in the pond a stone lantern and bronze cranes symbolize immortality, longevity and good fortune. Hakone is a tranquil garden which has attained additional atmosphere through age.

OPEN: Daily from 10 a.m. to 5 p.m. except on national holidays.

ADMISSION: Free.

ADDRESS: 21000 Big Basin Way, Saratoga, CA 95070.

MAINTAINED BY: City Parks Department, telephone 415-867-3438.

DIRECTIONS: From Stevens Creek Freeway (State 85) follow Saratoga-Sunnyvale Rd. to Saratoga and the junction of Big Basin Way. Hakone is less than a mile beyond.

Whittier

Japanese Garden in Rose Hills Memorial Park

This famous cemetery, well known for the beauty of its roses and fine landscaping, has an unusually lovely Japanese garden area as well. It adjoins the Lake of the Roses. The handsome dark wood bridge and *azumaya* (meditation shelter) are smaller replicas of ones in Ritsurin Park, in the Japanese city of Takamatsu. The garden was completed in 1963.

A very fine *Kasuga-Doro* lantern, moss-covered, eight feet tall, is over 300 years old. It was donated by the Japanese industrialist Mr. Tokugawa Narutaka. The small gravestones lie flat in the

Azumaya and bridge. (James L. McFadden)

well-manicured lawn, each marked with its name and dates and occasionally ornamented with delicate Japanese designs, or a line of poetry. Every stone has its vase of fresh flowers. Visiting this quiet resting place for Japanese-Americans, one senses the loving care of those who come here to sit by the water under the shade of fine old trees, surrounded by a truly Japanese garden.

On Memorial Day each year there are three separate ceremonies, the most colorful one being that of the Buddhist faith.

OPEN: Daily from 9 a.m. to sunset.

ADDRESS: Rose Hills Memorial Park, 3900 Workman Mill Rd., Whittier, CA 90601. Telephone: 213-699-0921.

DIRECTIONS: The Japanese Garden is in a section called Cherry Blossom Gardens, at the Lake of the Roses. Turn off Workman Hill Rd. onto Rose Hills Rd. and follow the sign. If in doubt, ask for a map at the information booth of Rose Hills Memorial Park, at the main entrance.

Colorado

Denver

Proposed Japanese Garden in Denver Botanic Gardens

This Japanese garden is still in the planning stage; work on it will probably begin in 1977. It will be located on two acres in the northwest corner of the Denver Botanic Gardens. A small stream runs through this section and will be part of the ornamental water system, widening into two or three small lagoons and providing locations for two little islands. The ground is already pleasantly rolling, ideal for a Japanese stroll garden.

This is the last portion of a ten-year project which is adding ten acres of new formal gardens to the existing areas which specialize in herbs, native plants and water gardens. The conservatory has a fine display of tropical plants and cacti.

OPEN: Denver Botanic Gardens are open weekdays, from 9 a.m. to 5 p.m.; weekends, 10 a.m. to 5 p.m. The Conservatory is open the same hours and also from 7-9 p.m. on Fridays. Picnic grounds in adjacent park.

ADMISSION: Free.

MAINTAINED BY: Denver Park and Recreation Department. Telephone: 303-297-2547.

DIRECTIONS: Go about 10 minutes east of downtown Denver via Colfax Ave., turn right on York St., then go 4 blocks to the entrance.

District of Columbia

Washington

U. S. National Arboretum

A new authentic Japanese garden has been added to this famous National Arboretum as a fitting entrance to the extraordinary collection of bonsai (miniature trees) donated by the Nippon Bonsai Association of Japan. This gift was made to the American people in commemoration of the bicentennial, and consists of fifty-three priceless bonsai, many 500 years old, from the collections of the emperor and his family and many high Japanese officials.

In order to give this unique display an appropriate setting, a long avenue of Japanese cryptomeria trees has been planted, leading to the walled Japanese garden (about 80' x 80'). This has been designed by Mr. Masao Kinoshita, a member of Hideo Sasaki Associates of Watertown, Mass. He has planned it as a quiet, small-scale approach to the lathe house beyond, where visitors will see the bonsai as a climax, in the manner of the introductory gardens leading to temples in Japan. The garden has carefully pruned trees of natural size, but all shrubs and plants are on a very small scale, to keep the controlled proportion in the bonsai tradition. The path leads past a small pool with *koi* (carp) and a few Japanese iris.

OPEN: (After July, 1976) 8 a.m. to 7 p.m. weekdays, Apr.-Oct.; 10 a.m. to 7 p.m. weekends. Winter months: 8 a.m. to 5 p.m. weekdays; 10 a.m. to 5 p.m. weekends.

ADDRESS: U.S. National Arboretum, 24th and R Sts., N.E., Washington, DC 20002. Telephone: 202-399-5400.

Washington

*Ippakutei, The Ceremonial Teahouse and Garden
at the Embassy of Japan*

The name *Ippakutei* is made from the reading of a combination of characters whose primary meaning, "virtue," complements its alternate meaning, "100th anniversary." The latter refers to the 1960 Centennial of Japan-United States relations, formally opened in 1860 when Japan's first embassy arrived in Washington to exchange ratifications of a Treaty of Amity and Commerce. Ippakutei was constructed in commemoration of this event. Former Ambassador Koichiro Asakai suggested that a ceremonial teahouse and garden might be built at the Embassy in Washington, and Japanese business leaders immediately began raising funds for the project through their Federation of Economic Organizations, the Japan Foreign Trade Council, and the Japan Chamber of Commerce and Industry.

The ceremonial teahouse was designed by the distinguished architectural scholar, Nahiko Emori. Prebuilt in Japan by the Kajima Construction Company of Tokyo, it was dismantled and shipped to the United States to be reconstructed by nine Kajima engineers and artisans. Since the building was to be used for exhibition, its design combined elements of both a Japanese home and a ceremonial teahouse. The entrance to the tea ceremony

room is only two feet square, so that guests entering must divest themselves of status and become humble and meditative in true Japanese tradition.

The garden, also designed by Mr. Emori, combines three representative styles. One style is an austere sand-and-rock Zen garden calculated to induce meditation; the second style resembles an early nineteenth-century garden in Matsue, designed by the great feudal lord and tea master, Fumai Matsudaire. One of its lanterns is of a type found at the Matsuo Shrine. The other lantern here is of the Sanko type, "the lantern of the three illuminations" whose openings represent the sun, moon and stars. The third style of garden approaches the teahouse with stones deliberately placed to slow the gait. This leads to a granite water basin for the purification of hands before taking part in the tea ceremony. A stone lantern here has the image of the Virgin Mary carved in the base, characteristic of the Oribe style, named after its designer who was a sixteenth-century Christian. These last two gardens are enclosed by a fence of square, openwork bamboo similar to that at the Kinkakuji in Kyoto.

OPEN: To visitors by appointment only, in groups limited to 30. Telephone: 202-234-2266. The guided tour takes 30 minutes, and is given only on Wednesdays between 2:30 and 4:30 p.m., in May, June, July, Sept. and Oct. but not in Aug. or on Japanese or American holidays. The teahouse and gardens are the only areas of the Embassy shown, and there is no tea ceremony or serving of refreshments. No children under 11 are admitted.

ADDRESS: 2520 Massachusetts Ave., N.W., Washington, DC 20008.

Florida

Delray Beach

Morikami Museum of Japanese History

This new Morikami Museum of Japanese History is a unique cultural contribution to America. Ground-breaking ceremonies were held in the fall of 1975, and it is expected to open in June 1976. It is situated on a small island in a man-made lake, surrounded by a simple Japanese garden with waterfalls, streams, pine trees and other evergreens, and is connected with the mainland by an Oriental-type bridge.

The forty acres for this new park and museum development were the gift of George S. Morikami. Born in 1885 in Japan, Mr. Morikami came to America at age twenty-one to farm pineapples in Florida. He is one of the few surviving members of the Yamoto Colony, once located in the Delray Beach-Boca Raton area. The park and museum are built in honor of Mr. Morikami and his fellow early settlers.

The museum, designed for the study of Japanese culture and horticulture, is in Japanese style inside and out. There are two bedrooms, a bath, kitchen, and a tearoom—just as a visitor might see them in Japan. The four other exhibit rooms display both

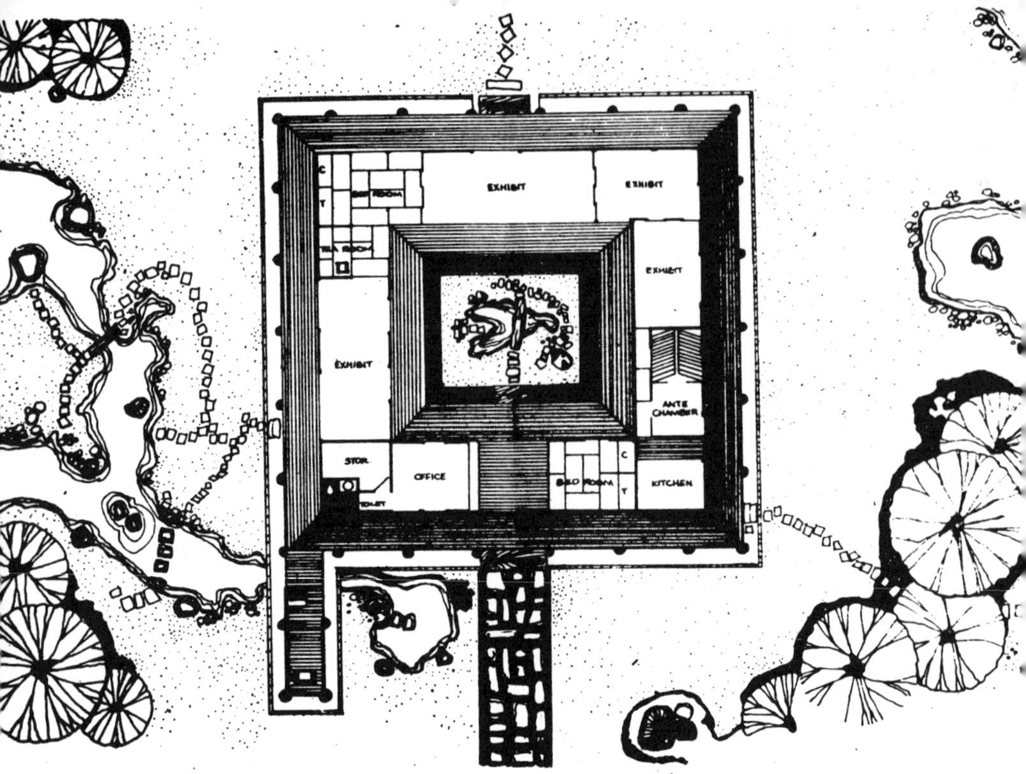

Plan of Museum of Japanese History and Japanese garden. (Palm Beach County Department of Parks and Recreation)

original artifacts and replicas of historical objects.

This is an unusual opportunity for Florida vacationers and citizens to explore a real Japanese house and its garden setting.

ADDRESS FOR INFORMATION: Palm Beach County Parks and Recreation Department, 5020 S. Congress Ave., Lake Worth, FL 33460. Telephone: 305-964-4420.

DIRECTIONS TO MUSEUM: Take Delray West Rd. east off the Florida Turnpike; turn right onto Carter Rd., which ends at Morikami Rd. and the Museum.

Miami

San-Ai-An Garden

San-Ai-An was the name chosen for this Japanese garden by its donor, the late wealthy industrialist Kiyoshi Ichimura, because these syllables stood for his guiding principles and loves: country, fellowman and work. When he first visited Miami in 1955, he was so charmed by the city that he told its officials he wanted to create an authentic Japanese garden for them to express friendship for the American people. Upon returning home, he began sending gifts: 500 orchid trees, a 300-year-old stone lantern, and an eight-ton, eight-foot-high granite statue of Hotei, the smiling Japanese god of prosperity.

In 1961 he shipped the materials for this one-acre garden. Included was the teahouse, the arbor for scholarly meditation (*azumaya*), three bridges and seven stone lanterns. Kingo Saka-moto, Japan's famous landscape architect, was sent over also with six carpenters and three gardeners to direct the garden's construction and work with some 100 city Parks Department employees.

The main gate is made of cypress wood and topped with Japanese tile. A zigzag bridge crosses the lagoon with its water lilies and carp. Near it is a dry stream carefully constructed of many rocks and plants. Feeding the shallow lagoon is a waterfall flowing over irregular stones. A stone pagoda, 15 feet tall and weighing 4½ tons, is a decorative feature.

The two-room teahouse is made of flawless natural bamboo, cedar and pine, with no knotholes, and without the use of a single nail. Near it is the waiting area within a bamboo fence, with a bench for guests, and at the house stands a stone purification basin. The entrance of the teahouse is traditionally small so that visitors must creep in humbly, and a twisted hemp shield divides the opening to be used by the nobility from that of the commoner. Mr. Ichimura dedicated the teahouse himself "with a prayer for the peace and happiness of all mankind." His was indeed a generous and touching gift of tranquility to a large, bustling American city.

OPEN: Daily 9 a.m. to 6 p.m.

ADMISSION: Free.

ADDRESS: MacArthur Causeway, Watson Island, Miami, FL 33100.

MAINTAINED BY: The City of Miami Parks and Recreation Department.

Above, infra-red photography creates a dramatic picture of the teahouse in the Japanese garden. Below, the azumaya. (Photos courtesy of Miami-Metro Department of Publicity of Tourism)

1. A Persian rug made of flowers in El Cerrito, California. (Sundar Shadi)

2. Looking up toward the shrine at U.C.L.A. Japanese garden, Los Angeles, California. (James L. McFadden)

3. Purification basin in the U.C.L.A. Japanese garden, Los Angeles, California. (Dorothy Loa McFadden)

4. Byodo-in Temple in Valley of the Temples, Oahu, Hawaii. (Dorothy Loa McFadden)

5. Below the red gate in the Japanese Tea Garden in Golden Gate Park, San Francisco, California. (Dorothy Loa McFadden)

6. The Chinese House in Heritage Village, Maui, Hawaii. (Dorothy Loa McFadden)

7. "Golden Shower Tree" and temple bell at Jodo Temple Garden in Lahaina, Maui, Hawaii. (Dorothy Loa McFadden)

8. The moon bridge at Huntington Botanical Gardens in San Marino, California. (Dorothy Loa McFadden)

Palm Beach

Chinese Garden at the Four-Arts Museum Library

What a beautiful reminder of old China! Here is a colorful yet restful example of the ancient Chinese courtyard garden. It is one of the small demonstration gardens planted on the grounds of the Society of Four-Arts in 1938 by members of the Garden Club of Palm Beach, an affiliate of the Garden Club of America. The Chinese Garden was designed by Mrs. Lorenzo Woodhouse and decorated by her with antique Chinese sculptures.

A moon gate opening in the wall near the entrance is filled in with an intricate wrought-iron grill, softly fringed with ferns above

White Foo Dog surrounded by azaleas, in the Chinese garden at the Four-Arts Museum Library. (Dorothy Loa McFadden)

and below. The openwork windows are of glazed tile. Stepping inside, one sees another ceramic ornamenting the wall—a jovial musician with cymbals. The plantings are restrained in Chinese fashion, with just enough greenery to set off the white Foo Dog statue, the yellow-and-green meditating Buddha, and the figures of two lovely goddesses: Kuan Yin, Goddess of Mercy, and Li Wong Tsen, Goddess of Gardens and Flowers. They are backed by more openwork tile of blue-green, and delicate shrimp plants. All these statues and decorations came from the Winter Palace Gardens in Peking, and are of the fifteenth and sixteenth centuries.

It seems very appropriate that the club member now in charge of this garden, Mrs. Robert I. Ballinger, Jr., breeds and shows Pekingese, the Chinese palace dogs. One of her champions is usually with her when she works in the garden, and undoubtedly feels right at home!

OPEN: Daily from 10 a.m. to 5 p.m., but closed Wed. afternoons during the winter, and on Sat. during the summer. The gardens are also open Sun. afternoons from Christmas to Easter. As this schedule is subject to change, it is advisable to telephone the library in advance of a visit: 305-655-2766.

ADMISSION: Free, by entering and getting permission in the library.

ADDRESS: Four-Arts Museum Library, Royal Palm Way, Palm Beach, FL 33480.

MAINTAINED BY: Members of the Garden Club of Palm Beach.

Hawaii

Hilo, Island of Hawaii

Liliuokalani Gardens Park

Liliuokalani Gardens Park, in spite of being named for a Hawaiian queen, is an authentic Japanese garden. Now covering

Left, Buddha statue in Chinese garden at Four-Arts Museum Library. (Dorothy Loa McFadden)

twenty-four acres, it is quite large and very beautiful. *Reader's Digest* listed it in its 1974 "Treasures of America." Like the legendary phoenix so revered by the Japanese, this garden has been destroyed a number of times by the elements but has always arisen again to new beauty.

The idea for such a park was first conceived by Mrs. C. C. Kennedy, wife of a Hilo businessman, after a visit to Japan in 1914. She thought that the Waiakea fish ponds near the harbor would make an ideal location. Eventually this land was set aside for park use by the Territory, and Mr. Kennedy made the initial donation toward its creation. Yamamoto, a local contractor expert in Japanese gardens, drew the plans. The first stone lantern was the gift of the Hilo Shinkokai, a Japanese women's society. Bit by bit, swamp land was drained, plantings were made, the pond and channels became features on an undulating terrain ornamented with ledges of old "pahoehoe lava" left by earlier volcanic eruptions. This island is composed of five volcanic mountains, some still active.

Yet it was not a flow of lava but a tremendous tidal wave produced by seismic disturbances elsewhere which, in April 1946, completely destroyed the Japanese garden as well as a great many of Hilo's coastal buildings. The original fisherman's shrine was swept away, stone lanterns toppled into deep mud, trees broke and fell. The ponds were left filled with dangerous barracuda from the ocean. While the work of restoration was still under way in 1953, the barracuda were too well fed on mullet to be tempted by baited hooks and they finally had to be shot. The pagoda and bridges, meanwhile, had fallen prey to termites and needed replacing. Eventually the garden was restored to its original beauty.

Then in 1960 another tidal wave almost destroyed the whole garden. Now Hilo's famous 442nd Veterans' Club became interested in the restoration. Members volunteered their time and labor in putting together those few broken stone lanterns which could be found. New designing and planting was undertaken by landscape architect N. Nakani of Kyoto. Finally in 1968, in commemoration of the centennial of Japanese immigration to the Hawaiian Islands, gifts for the Japanese garden came from many sources: stone lanterns from the home prefectures from which immigrants had come; a lantern from Hilo's Sister City Oshima, donated by the mayor, and a *torii* from Oshima Island itself; a pair

Above, the red-roofed bridge; below, stone Chinese lion-dog; overleaf, the pond in Liliuokalani Gardens Park. (James L. McFadden)

of stone lions from the city of Nagasaki; and another lantern which was the gift of the governor of metropolitan Tokyo. When all was ready, Kinsaku Nakani, professor at Kyoto University and a landscape architect, came to Hilo to place all these artifacts correctly. These were then dedicated by Prince Hitachi, youngest son of Emperor Hirohito, and the Prince's wife Hanako. In 1972 an authentic tea ceremony house was added. It was the gift of Shoshitsu Sen, grand master of the Uransenke School of Tea Ceremony in Kyoto, who came to Hilo to dedicate it in person.

This is a particularly spacious, tranquil garden, its many beautiful features so carefully separated that there is no crowding in of detail. The pools of clear water are planted with water lilies and lotus. In one area, Nagao Sakurai, noted landscape architect, designed a traditional dry Zen Garden of meditation, using rocks to simulate a waterfall and white sand for a "cool mountain stream." The red moon bridge and a delightful scarlet-roofed bridge in another section are colorful accents. The other bridges are of stone, and the plantings and black lava rocks give a muted and unified effect. The stone purification basin at the teahouse is the only thing left today from the ancient shrine on this spot, to which fishermen came from nearby Waiakea-town to pray for a good catch before heading out to sea.

OPEN: Daily.

ADMISSION: Free.

ADDRESS: At Banyan Drive and Lihiwai Street, not far from the harbor.

MAINTAINED BY: The Department of Parks and Recreation of the county of Hawaii. Telephone: 808-961-8311.

Kepaniwai Park, Maui

Heritage Gardens

The Heritage Gardens were built as a tribute to the ethnic groups which settled on Maui. Among them, visitors to Hawaii may enjoy a bit of old China and Japan. Nestled below a glorious mountain range are six typical small houses surrounded with traditional gardens: an early Hawaiian thatched hut with a taro patch and Kukui trees; a white New England cottage commemorating the early American missionaries; a Filipino house of woven bamboo in a jungle setting; a Portuguese house with a long pergola, pools and a formal flower garden; and the Chinese and Japanese houses and gardens. All were designed by Richard C. Tongg, ASLA.

The white Chinese house—imported from China—has attractive red trim and a blue-tiled roof turning up at the corners. Windows and railings are of handsome grilled design. In front is a small pond and narrow canals, lined with worn coral to simulate the traditional Chinese marble. The white blossoms of *spathiphyllum* line the banks. Chinese rice flower, cinnamon tree, lychee, fishpole bamboo, willow and Chinese pine are among the native plantings which give this garden its authenticity. A blue-and-white bridge topped with red railings leads on to the next garden.

The Japanese house is reached through a small roofed gateway flanked by hedges. The building is charming and authentic, having been imported from Japan. Beyond lies a hill-and-pond garden, the water winding in and out among rocks and under a bridge. A tall stone pagoda and lanterns of various types seem almost white against the dark evergreens. Unfortunately there is an over-abundance of visible concrete binding stones together in paths and for the rim of the pond. This destroys the effect of "nature untouched by man" which is so essential in a traditional Japanese garden.

The idea behind these Heritage Gardens is a splendid one, the choice of authentic plant material for each country scrupulously done. Their setting below the mist-capped mountains at the entrance to the famous Iao Valley is breathtakingly beautiful.

OPEN: Daily. Picnic area included.

ADMISSION: Free.

DIRECTIONS: Follow Highway 32 from Wailuku to Kepaniwai Park. (This is usually a preliminary stop on bus tours going to the famous Iao Needle, a 2250-foot pointed rock rising from the valley floor.)

The Chinese house. (James L. McFadden)

The Japanese garden in Heritage Gardens, Maui. (James L. McFadden)

Lahaina, Maui

Jodo Cultural Garden

The Jodo Cultural Garden is a Japanese Buddhist temple complex, built and owned by the Lahaina Jodo Mission. Although there is no extensive garden, there are quite a few flowers. The long hedge of oleanders, the tall slender cypresses at the entrance, and the glorious yellow "shower tree" *(cassia)* drooping over the bell tower—all are reminiscent of Oriental gardens (see color plate). The buildings were completed in 1970, and are dedicated to all the Mission's loved ones who had passed away during the last 100 years.

The color design of the authentic Buddhist temple was done by a Lahaina artist, Tadashi Sato. Inside are five paintings by Hajin Iwasaki, a noted Japanese artist. Both the temple and pagoda are roofed with pure copper. On the first floor of the pagoda are niches for ashes of the deceased, and a small altar. On a high stone platform there is a great Buddha of copper and bronze, said to be the largest of its kind outside of Japan. It was cast in Kyoto by the Venerable Mitsuo Sato, head priest of Kamakura Daibutsu Temple. It stands 8 feet high and weighs about 3½ tons. Seated against a background of Maui's beautiful mountains, it is an inspiring sight.

The great bell hanging in the tower is also made of bronze and weighs about 3000 pounds. It is inscribed in Chinese characters with the words: "The Centennial Memorial Bell for the first Japanese immigrants to Hawaii." On the other side is the Jodo prayer, and the names of many donors and supporters of the Mission. This bell is rung eleven times each evening at 8 o'clock. The first three rings are for "I go to the Buddha for guidance; I go to the Dhamma (the teachings of Buddha) for guidance; I go to the Sangha (brotherhood) for guidance." The next eight rings represent the eight-fold pathway to righteousness: right understanding, purpose, speech, conduct, livelihood, endeavor, thought and meditation.

Entrance to the Jodo Cultural Garden. (James L. McFadden)

OPEN: Daily.

ADMISSION: Free.

ADDRESS: On Puunoa Point, about one-half mile from the business center of Lahaina.

Honolulu

Japanese and Chinese Gardens at Honolulu International Airport

Honolulu International Airport is one of the ten busiest airports in the United States. Yet the designers included something unique for the enjoyment of passengers and visitors: a garden area covering some 30,000 square feet, planted as a Japanese garden on one side, a Chinese garden on the other. They were designed by Richard C. Tongg, ASLA, and completed in 1962.

The gardens lie directly behind the main building. Thousands of

The Japanese garden at Honolulu Airport. (Tongg Associates)

people have already walked through them and sat relaxed in the open pavilions during long hours of boring waits for plane arrivals and departures. What a joy to be out under Hawaii's blue skies and sunshine instead of sitting on a hard bench inside the terminal waiting rooms!

The Japanese garden has a traditional zigzag bridge, designed to foil pursuing evil spirits who were said to run only along straight lines. This crosses a pool filled with colorful *koi* (carp). There are ornamental stone lanterns and a fine ornamental stone pagoda along the path which leads to a simple *azumaya* (meditation pavilion).

In the Chinese garden, two arched moon bridges lead visitors over the irregular pool, the home of friendly ducks. The pavilion here is covered with a golden-tiled roof set on slender red pillars. Nearby stands a bronze life-sized statue of Sun Yat Sen, donated by the Republic of China, Taiwan. A marble railing of Oriental design encloses the gardens.

The Chinese garden at Honolulu Airport. (Photo Hawaii)

Honolulu

Japanese Garden at East-West Center, University of Honolulu

The Japanese Garden is located behind the Jefferson Hall administration building of the East-West Center. Covering about 3/4 of an acre, it was landscaped in the traditional Japanese style by Kenzo Ogata of Tokyo, who was assisted by nine other landscape architects from seven nations. It was created by the East-West Center and twenty-two Japanese business members of the Federation of Economic Organizations in Tokyo, which did the original financing. The garden, completed in 1963, was formally presented to the Center by Taizo Ishizaka, president of this federation. In 1964 a "coral shower tree" *(cassia)* was planted in the garden by Prince Akihito and Princess Michiko of Japan. A willow branch cut by Emperor Hirohito on the Imperial Palace grounds has now grown into a fine willow tree.

Since the garden borders Manoa stream, it was used for creating three levels joined by small waterfalls. Its progress symbolizes to the Japanese the life of man, beginning in a fast moving turmoil, steadying in adulthood, and slowing down during old age. The pond created by the stream is in the design of the Japanese character for "heartfelt greeting." More than 100 colorful *koi* (carp) were placed in the water by the Hawaii Goldfish and Carp Association in a traditional "hold and release" Japanese ceremony.

Near the highest waterfall is a nine-tiered stone pagoda, and along the stream are two stone lanterns: one is the "snow-reflecting" type; the other, a 400-year-old traveler's lantern. There is a small teahouse with the traditional water-purification basin in the shape of a Chinese coin with a bamboo spout. Plants suitable for a warm-temperate zone climate were substituted for the traditional Japanese species, but were carefully chosen and are kept well pruned for the needed restrained Japanese effect. This is a very tranquil spot of quiet repose for Center and University students and visitors alike, and an inspiring example of East-West cooperation. In its own way it is fulfilling the purpose of the East-West Center, where students from many parts of the world gather to help promote better relations and understanding among the peoples of the United States, Asia and the Pacific area through cooperative study, training and research.

OPEN: Daily, dawn to dusk. An interesting folder about the Japanese Garden may be obtained in Jefferson Hall. It lists all the plants in the garden on detailed plans.

ADMISSION: Free.

ADDRESS: East-West Center, 1777 East-West Rd., Manoa Campus, University of Honolulu, Honolulu, HI 96822. Telephone: 808-948-7700.

Pond area in the Japanese garden, East-West Center. (James L. McFadden)

Honolulu

Oriental Courtyard, Honolulu Academy of Arts

The Oriental Courtyard of this famous museum is one of five planted inner courts. It is surrounded by walls of different heights, reminiscent of the traditional Chinese courtyard gardens, and its plantings of bamboo and small trees are also in the restrained Chinese tradition. A strange fountainhead of Oriental origin set into one red wall is a lion-like fanciful beast from whose open mouth water flows into a small pool. Here and there are tropical flowers in ornamental Chinese pots. The courtyard is always a beautiful, restful place, a perfect complement to the outstanding Oriental exhibits in the museum.

OPEN: From 10 a.m. to 4:30 p.m. Tues. through Sat., and from 2 to 5 p.m. on Sun. Closed Mon. Sandwich luncheons are served in the Garden Cafe of the Academy Tues. through Fri., 11:45 a.m. to 1:30 p.m., by the Academy Volunteers Council. Closed July and Aug. Reservations are necessary.

ADMISSION: Free.

ADDRESS: 900 S. Beretania St., Honolulu, HI 96814. Telephone: 808-538-3693.

DIRECTIONS: No. 2 bus from Waikiki takes 15 minutes; or take No. 1 or No. 2 bus from downtown to corner of King St. and Ward St.

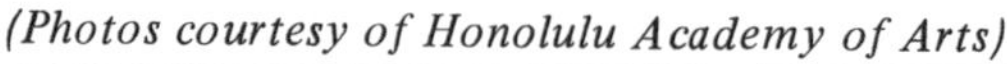

(Photos courtesy of Honolulu Academy of Arts)

Honolulu

Japanese Gardens at Soto-Zen Mission Temple

Several small Japanese Gardens have been planted around this interesting Zen-Buddhist temple. A narrow one borders the building, under the balcony with its Oriental openwork railing. Another larger one is at the side, landscaped with an artificial mound decorated by a stone pagoda. Below this is a small pond and curved bridge. A stone statue and lovely openwork pagoda-lantern five stories high nestle against a background of trees and shrubs which try to shield the little garden from surrounding skyscrapers. In another section there is a narrow Zen stone-and-gravel meditation garden. In back, a collection of bonsai—dwarf trees—is arranged for inspection.

The Soto-Zen Mission Temple and its gardens are open to visitors. The building's architecture was inspired by the Gaya Temple in India, its octagonal towers representing stages in Buddha's way of life. The beautiful interior, however, with its rich gold and red ornamental altar, is Japanese. Visitors will be wel-

comed any morning by the Buddhist priest who will explain the fundamentals of his religion, and the details inside the temple.

ADDRESS: 1708 Nuuanu Ave., Honolulu, Hawaii.

Honolulu

Kyoto Gardens, Honolulu Memorial Park

Kyoto Gardens in Honolulu Memorial Park is a very beautiful cemetery for those of the Buddhist faith and others who believe in cremation. Two historical temples of Japan, completed in 1966, have been recreated here. One is the Kinkaku-ji, the famous "Golden Pavilion" of Kyoto, originally built in 1394 partly as a home and partly as a temple to hold the relics of Buddha received from Emperor T'ai-tsu of China; it is topped by a golden phoenix,

symbol of everlasting life. The second is the Sanju or three-tiered pagoda (sixteenth century) of Minami Hokko-ji Temple outside of Nara. Both are used in these replicas as columbariums for urns containing ashes of the deceased, and both have revolving altars for symbols of the various Buddhist faiths and the Christian Cross, so that any officiating minister can stand before his own appropriate background. The pagoda, 116 feet tall, is painted in bright coral, mustard, white and turquoise, topped with a blue-green roof and copper spire. There are ten other small cinerariums on the grounds, all in Japanese-style architecture.

Surrounding the "Golden Pavilion" is the Mirror Lake Garden, fashioned after the Muromachi style. It was designed by Kinsaku Nakame, professor at Kyoto University and a leading landscape authority, with Patrick Oka, a former pupil. Within the lake a special rock represents the nine mountains and eight seas of the Buddhist mythological paradise. A bridge connecting the pavilion to shore extends over Crane Island to Tortoise Island, both symbols of longevity. A waterfall, spring, rocks, islets—all are reminiscent of the gardens of the original pavilion in Kyoto, but on a much smaller scale. There are many Hawaiian flowers on the grounds, but it is hoped eventually that there may be a different blossoming scene in each of the four seasons as there is in Japan. In ever-blooming Hawaii this would mean bougainvilleas for winter, azaleas for spring, the cassia ("golden shower tree") for summer, chrysanthemums and poinsettias for fall. Some 300 carp were released into the waters by donors in a ceremony during the dedication.

OPEN: Daily.

OWNED AND MAINTAINED BY: Honolulu Memorial Park, Inc., 22 Craigside Pl., Honolulu, HI 96817. Telephone: 808-536-9364.

Honolulu

Oriental Garden, Alice Cooke Spalding House

The Oriental-Hawaiian Garden at this house, which is an extension of the Honolulu Academy of Arts, is an interesting horticul-

Left, pagoda in Kyoto Gardens. (Kyoto Gardens)

Above left, Chinese stone horse of the Ming period; right, ancient stone stele; below, glazed tile wall and figure. (Photos by James L. McFadden)

tural and ornamental combination of East and West. The terrace is Hawaiian, covered with lawn and surrounded by fine old tropical trees, but its decorations are all Chinese. A life-sized pair of sturdy white stone horses of the Ming period prance on the grass at one end. Near the pepper tree there is a stone stele carved with Buddhist figures. A statue of Kuan Yin, Goddess of Mercy, is from the sixth or seventh century. Two marble statues called "Young Beauties" date from the nineteenth century. Along one side of the terrace a low wall is decorated with glazed Chinese tiles in high relief, with standing figures at each end, flowers, birds and beasts between. Here and there one sees garden sculptures of rabbits, frogs, cranes and other animals. None of these objects are great works of art, but they lend an Oriental air to this upper area.

Below this is a Hawaiian version of a Japanese stroll garden. It was designed between 1928 and 1941 by the Reverend K. H. Inagaki, a Japanese Christian minister and garden enthusiast living in Hawaii. Its Hawaiian name is *Nuumealani* meaning "heavenly terraces," as it descends by easy stages into a valley. Inagaki planned it as "a retreat where one may escape to meditate and experience harmony." As in the old traditional Chinese landscape gardens and later in the hill-and-water stroll gardens in Japan, the element of surprise is paramount as the path winds down from one small scene to another. One never sees too far ahead. Each part has a bench for contemplation of the particular beauties of carefully chosen rocks, representing at times an imaginary waterfall or a dry streambed, and the exotic flowers and trees around them. It is a jungle garden of plants from every tropical area of the world, each part of the stroll having much of horticultural interest—a Western idea—as well as being a scene for quiet contemplation as is usual in the gardens of China and Japan.

The Alice Cooke Spalding House contains changing exhibitions of Asian arts, which supplement those in the Honolulu Academy of Arts, and also the permanent collection of some 5000 Japanese woodblock prints donated by James A. Michener.

OPEN: Tues. through Sun., 1-4:30 p.m. Closed Mon. Tours by trained volunteer guides from the Garden Club of Honolulu, the Outdoor Circle and the Federated Garden Clubs are offered by appointment between 9 and 11:30 a.m., each tour of house and gardens, or the gardens alone, taking about 1½ hours. Shorter tours called "A Walk Through the Garden" may also be arranged for the afternoons. Telephone: 537-9088.

ADMISSION: Adults $1.00, military 50¢, students 25¢; academy members, children under 12, and student groups with instructors, free. Tues., admission free to all.

ADDRESS: 2411 Makiki Dr., Honolulu, HI 96822.

Honolulu

Banyan Court in the Lester McCoy Pavilion

The original Banyan Court in Ala Moana Park was designed in the 1930s with evident Hindu inspiration. The newly reconstructed area, although very modern in conception, still retains the fine sense of proportion and quiet use of space so beloved in the gardens and courtyards of India.

The Banyan Court is only a part of the $1.5 million Pavilion complex, a memorial from his wife to Lester McCoy, Honolulu philanthropist and orchid expert. It includes meeting rooms, offices, indoor and outdoor stages, and an open lanai dining area. Everything is spacious—the court alone is approximately 160 by 220 feet.

Four superb old specimens of banyan trees (the true *Ficus benghalensis* from India) are the dominant features of the courtyard. In the daytime they provide much welcome shade with dappled sunlight; they are spectacularly floodlighted at night. The stone flooring is laid in intricate irregular patterns of several muted colors. Two large pools edged in sweeping free-form curves fill the center of the court, while others are placed in the corners, interspersed with flowerbeds of varying shapes. Stepped copings with dignified, solid ornamentation frame all of these units. Large earthenware urns make accents here and there. Conceived by Charles J. W. Chamberland, AIA, this is an inspired combination of modern architecture with a timeless Oriental flavor.

The famous Honolulu Outdoor Circle, well known for its many efforts in beautifying the city, was asked to plan the selection of

Banyan Court in Ala Moana Park. (Honolulu Department of Parks and Recreation)

flowers and small shrubs. The Department of Parks and Recreation can well be proud of this new addition to Ala Moana Park, which was only opened in the fall of 1975.

OPEN: Daily.

ADMISSION: Free.

ADDRESS: Department of Parks and Recreation, 650 S. King St., Honolulu, HI 96813. Telephone: 808-523-4211.

Valley of the Temples, Oahu

Byodo-in Temple

Here a person would truly believe he was in Japan! A Japanese garden of seven acres surrounds this temple which is an almost exact replica of Byodo-in in Uji, Japan, near Kyoto. The original structure, now over 900 years old, is an example of the best

religious architecture of the period when the Fujiwara family was in full sway. This red and white replica has been placed in an even more dramatic setting than its prototype, with some of Oahu's most beautiful mountains as a background. The temple in Hawaii is said to have cost 2.6 million dollars from private funds. It was opened to the public in 1969.

Entrance to the garden is over a typical red bridge crossing part of the reflecting pool which surrounds the main building. At the left is a wooden tower holding the decorative three-ton brass bell with its horizontal bamboo striker. Beyond is a small waterfall and a Meditation House for quiet contemplation, set on a high mound. The temple building, like its original in Japan, is designed to represent the legendary phoenix with wings spread, the rear wing being its tail. At the peak of its gracefully curved roof stand two brass phoenixes, male and female, symbols of everlasting life. The great statue of Amida, Buddha of the Western Paradise, sits inside the open door of the temple. Carved of wood by Japanese sculptor

(Photos by James L. McFadden)

Masazo Inui and covered with gold and lacquer, it is said to be the largest wooden Buddha created in the last 900 years. From the platform surrounding the temple, one gets a fine view of the simple plantings, mainly the starry white blossoms of crape jasmine *(ervatamia coronaria)* edging the curves of the reflecting pool (see color plate). Some 2000 *koi* (carp) crowd the waters. A traditional Japanese teahouse stands at the far side, serving as a refreshment booth and gift shop.

OPEN: Daily including Sunday, from 8 a.m. to 5 p.m.

ADMISSION: $1.00, which is collected at a booth on the approaching road by a pretty Japanese girl in kimono.

ADDRESS FOR INFORMATION: Valley of the Temples Memorial Park, 47-200 Kahekili Highway, Kaneohe, Hawaii. Telephone: 808-239-8811.

DIRECTIONS: From Honolulu drive through the Wilson Tunnel, turn left onto Kahekili Highway for 3 miles, then left again to the Valley of the Temples entrance.

Illinois

Decatur

Oriental Garden in Scovill Gardens Park

This Oriental garden is part of Scovill Gardens Park, a gift from Mr. and Mrs. Guy Scovill. Hundreds of Oriental art objects had been collected by the Scovills on their travels, which were formerly housed in a Chinese pavilion on their estate, a summer home on the shore of Lake Decatur. Now most of these ornaments are on display in the Science Hall of Millikin University, Decatur.

In January 1948, they gave Scovill Gardens to the Decatur Park District. The Oriental garden, about ¼ acre in size, was designed by Jack Swing of the University of Illinois, and opened to the public in 1965. There are some Japanese lanterns and azaleas, pines, and a number of flowering trees.

OPEN: Daily from 7:30 a.m. to 4 p.m.

ADDRESS: 71 S. Country Club Rd., Decatur, IL 62521. For information: Decatur Park District, Mueller Park, Decatur, IL 62521. Telephone: 217-422-5911.

Glencoe

Proposed Japanese Gardens of Chicago Horticultural Society

Three Japanese gardens are being built here in the Botanic Garden of the Chicago Horticultural Society. They have been designed by a well-known landscape architect, Professor Koichi Kawana, of the University of California at Los Angeles.

The gardens will be located on three islands, having a total area of about 4½ acres, in the large lake which is one of the main features of this botanic garden. Though still under construction, it is hoped that it will be completed some time in 1977.

OPEN: The Botanic Garden of the Chicago Horticultural Society is open from 9 a.m. to 6 p.m. in summer, and 9 a.m. to 4 p.m. in winter.

ADMISSION: There may be an admission fee in the future.

ADDRESS: 775 Dundee Rd., Glencoe, IL 60022. Mail: Chicago Horticultural Society, P.O. Box 90, Glencoe, IL 60022. Telephone: 312-835-5360.

DIRECTIONS: From Chicago, take John F. Kennedy Expressway

The water color rendering for the proposed Japanese Gardens at the Botanic Garden of the Chicago Horticultural Society, made by their designer, Prof. Koichi Kawana. (Photo by Philip D. Decker)

(Rte. 94) north. Then take Lake-Cook exit and proceed east ¼ mile to the garden.

Indiana

Michigan City

International Friendship Gardens

Here one may see typical gardens of seventeen nations—a horticultural trip around the world! The International Friendship

Gardens originated at the Century of Progress Exposition in Chicago in 1934. After this closed, the gardens were recreated on their present site of over 100 acres, as a private, nonprofit project. Hundreds of distinguished persons from around the globe were charter members—presidents, kings, queens, governors, artists, musicians and scientists. All were dedicated to this symbol of international friendship, unity and understanding.

Each garden was planned to show the traditional design and flowers of its homeland. King George V of England sent one of his own gardeners to start the English garden; Queen Wilhelmina donated thousands of tulips, and the Netherlands have continued this gift every year since. There are traditional gardens of America, Australia, Canada, England, France, Germany, Greece, Holland, Italy, Norway, Poland, Scotland, Sweden, Switzerland and Turkey. Two Oriental gardens are included: a Chinese garden with fine willow trees, two stone lions, and a simple bridge over a pond; and the Persian garden, a patterned group of rose beds with a few

Guardian lion under a willow tree in the Chinese garden, part of the International Friendship Gardens. (James Paul McFadden)

Persian urns. At the dedication, Mr. M. A. Foranghi, prime minister of Persia, said, "It seems to me that in the worship of Beauty and Art, all the world is unanimous."

It is sad to report that the once enthusiastic support of these lovely gardens seems to have vanished. Hundreds of visitors arrive every year from all parts of the world, interested in seeing the gardens and particularly those of their own countries. Yet the lack of adequate financial support with a resulting cutback in services has inevitably led to deterioration. The only income for the gardens is derived from admission fees and rentals of the two music stages for local festivals and a garden for weddings. Hopefully, our garden clubs and individual garden lovers will do something to restore this fine project to its former beauty.

OPEN: Daily from May 11 to Oct., 9 a.m. to 5 p.m.

ADMISSION: $2.00 for adults; $1.00 for children 6 to 12.

ADDRESS: Pottawattomie Park, Rte. 12. Mail: International Friendship Gardens Music Festivals, Inc., Michigan City, IN 46360. Telephone: 219-874-3664.

DIRECTIONS: Follow US 12 eastward from Michigan City about 1½ miles; turn right on Liberty Trail and follow signs.

Louisiana

Avery Island

Chinese Garden in the Jungle Gardens

This Chinese garden is only a small part (four acres) of the beautiful Jungle Gardens created by Mr. E. A. McIlhenny on his ancestral island estate. He was particularly interested in growing camellias, and when he died in 1949 it was estimated that there were over 600 cultivars on the island, many developed by him from imports from China, Japan and Europe. A large number of these are planted along the pond in front of the colorful bamboo pagoda with its historic bronze Buddha. This statue was built in China by Chen-Ha-Chin for the Shonfa Temple northeast of Peking, by order of Emperor Hui-Tsung (1101-1125). In the early 1900s the temple was looted by a rebel general who sent it to New York to be sold. There, friends of Mr. McIlhenny saw it, and bought it for him as a gift. A large well-designed *torii* serves as an entrance and frame for the temple.

The tranquility of the great live oaks with their festoons of Spanish moss, and the reflection of the temple and statue in the water, lend a truly Oriental atmosphere to this southern American garden. This was expressed by its owner in his poem:

Left, stone bridge and lagoon in the Chinese garden. (Avery Island) Right, the ancient bronze Buddha statue. (Pauline Crittenden)

BUDDHA SPEAKS

*Peacefully I rest upon this lagoon's
bank as pale green bamboos sway above
my throne.*

*Clouds of blossoms soften the sifted
light falling golden and misty through
the boughs above.*

*Long days of travel brought me from
my home, yet I have known
no hour of calmer rest.*

*My thoughts are like the swaying
bamboo's crest
waved to and fro
above the rippling stream,*

*Clear and blue
as from a glorious Dream.*

—E.A. McIlhenny

The Chinese garden was designed by Owen Southwell, Louisiana architect, and A. A. Hunt, landscape architect, and was opened to the public in 1942. The 300-acre Jungle Gardens include the famous bamboo "apartments" built over the water to save the egret from extinction. Here many hundreds of these beautiful birds now hatch their young and return each year after migration. The gardens are a memorial to one of America's great naturalists.

OPEN: Daily from 8 a.m. to 5 p.m.

ADMISSION: $1.75 for adults, 75c for children 6 to 12.

ADDRESS: Jungle Gardens, Avery Island, LA 70513. Telephone: 318-364-8184.

DIRECTIONS: Turn off toll road SR 329.

Jefferson Island, New Iberia

Rip Van Winkle's Live Oak Gardens

The serenely beautiful Japanese garden is only a small part of these twenty acres called Rip Van Winkle's Live Oak Gardens. Its main feature is a fine teahouse designed by Hal N. Perkins. It was named *Tsubaki-An* (camellia pavilion) because of the many fine camellias growing around it. These had been given to the owner, J. Lyle Bayless, Jr., when he was a young man, by his horticultural mentor, E. A. McIlhenny (see Avery Island, La.). The redwood walls and doors of the teahouse were smoothly finished, but its supporting posts were deliberately kept rough, to blend into the natural stone footings. Similarly, the plantings used close to the house are low and soft-textured, while larger, coarser ones are used at a greater distance, thus gradually blending into the natural landscape. The garden was designed by Michael A. Richard after a globe-circling trip with Mr. Bayless, when both were particularly

The teahouse, Tsubaki-An. *(Live Oak Gardens)*

charmed by the gardens of Japan. The pool, planted with Japanese iris, is crossed by a path made of millstones collected in many parts of the world. This is a muted, peaceful garden in the true Japanese spirit.

Rip Van Winkle's Live Oak Gardens have been designated a National Historical Landmark by the U.S. Department of the Interior, because the land and house formerly belonged to the world-famous actor Joseph Jefferson. His title role in Washington Irving's play *Rip Van Winkle* had made him beloved throughout the world for forty years. In 1870 he designed and built the house to which many dignitaries came for visits, including President Grover Cleveland. There is a two-mile long alley of live oaks; and six lovely flower gardens of many types, including an Elizabethan knot garden and a cascade inspired by famous originals in England.

OPEN: Daily from 9 a.m. to 5 p.m.

ADMISSION: $2.25 for adults, $1.00 for children 4 to 16, children under 4 free. Picnic area. The house is not open to the public. Plants grown in the gardens and greenhouse may be purchased at the entrance.

MAIL ADDRESS: Rip Van Winkle's Live Oak Gardens, P.O. Box 234, New Iberia, LA 70560. Telephone: 318-365-3631.

DIRECTIONS: Gardens are 7 miles southwest of New Iberia on highways 675 and 14.

Maine

Mount Desert Island, Northeast Harbor

Asticou Azalea Gardens

A Japanese garden of the dry Zen type for quiet meditation is a part of this lovely place in which the native plants and local stones

The dry sand-and-stone meditation garden. (George Taloumis)

of Maine make a fitting natural setting. Asticou Azalea Gardens were designed by Charles K. Savage with financial backing by John D. Rockefeller, Jr. A rough stone lantern on a rock in the pond, and a curved stone bridge over a small waterfall already hint at an Oriental atmosphere as one approaches the Japanese garden.

There, benches are arranged in a semi-circle enclosed by shrubs, where visitors may sit and quietly study the rocks in their "sea" of sand raked into wave patterns. All around is the fragrance of Maine pines, heather, native swamp laurel and Labrador tea.

Mr. Savage had an innate feeling for nature. "The brook and lake were here," he once said. "The plants and the stones let you know where they want to go." He had the instincts of a Japanese garden designer.

The pond and stone bridge at Asticou Azalea Gardens. (George Taloumis)

OPEN: Daily.

ADMISSION: Free.

MAIL ADDRESS: Asticou Azalea Gardens, Box 187, Northeast Harbor, ME 04662. Telephone: 207-276-5456.

DIRECTIONS: By car, turn off U.S. 1 at Ellsworth onto State Rte. 3 to Mt. Desert Island. Follow Rte. 198 almost to Northeast Harbor, but turn left onto Rte. 3 to Asticou Azalea Gardens.

Maryland

Wheaton

Brookside Garden

Brookside Garden is a lovely new park with Japanese influences apparent in its design. Opened in 1974, it was planned by landscape architect Hans Hanses on a ½-acre island in a lake. Bridges and other ornamental features will be added gradually. The entrance gate is of rough dark wood in the familiar *torii* design. This leads to a viewing pavilion at the water's edge, banked with azaleas. Japanese black pines and Japanese maples add color contrast among the trees.

OPEN: 8 a.m. to 5 p.m. every day.

ADMISSION: Free.

ADDRESS: Glenallen Ave., Wheaton, MD 20902. Mail address: The Maryland-National Capital Park & Planning Commission, 8787 Georgia Ave., Silver Spring, MD 20907. Telephone: 301-589-1480.

Oriental gate at Brookside Garden. (Bob Rinker)

Massachusetts

Edgartown

"Mi Toi" Japanese Garden

This lovely three-acre Japanese garden is privately owned, but open to the public at all times. It was originally planned by the late Hugh Jones, an architect who lived in Japan for some time after World War II. He designed the house in typical Japanese fashion on the outside with sliding walls and a "moon window," but he made the interior comfortable with Western conveniences. After his death the property was bought by Mrs. Seth Wakeman, who lived in the house for some years, but now uses it only for occasional parties or as a private retreat.

The garden is simple, mainly covered with the native pitch pine so similar to those which grow in Japan. Two small waterfalls feed into a brook and ponds which are bordered with Japanese iris and primroses (*Primula japonica*). Between mid-April and mid-May when these are in bloom, together with some 5000 naturalized daffodils and various rhododendrons, the garden presents a gay, colorful picture. Yet at every other season, even when covered with snow, the place radiates a serene Oriental beauty immediately evident to visitors. There is no ostentation, no ornamentation. Just the sense of lovely nature untouched by man, which is the ultimate aim of every true Japanese garden designer.

OPEN: The garden is open daily; the house only by appointment, by telephoning Mr. John R. Perkins, 617-627-5338.

ADMISSION: Free.

ADDRESS: Dyke Rd., Chappaquidick Island, Edgartown, MA 02539. Mail: P.O. Box 588.

DIRECTIONS: Take the little ferry from Edgartown for 4 minutes (price 75¢) to Chappaquidick Island. Garden is right on Dyke Rd.

Japanese garden at Edgartown. (John R. Perkins)

Salem

Japanese Garden at Peabody Museum of Salem

The Japanese garden at this famous maritime museum can be enjoyed by anyone from the sidewalk, looking through the iron fence. So it is a "viewing garden," not a "stroll garden." It was designed about 1960 by Mr. Oliver Wolcott, a trustee of the museum, and Mrs. Cornelius Crane. Although it is only fifty feet square, it seems larger because of its spacious placement of shrubs and trees bordering the graveled area. There is a lovely Moraine locust, flowering crabs, Korean dogwoods, and many other appropriate plantings.

The beautiful bronze lantern was a gift from Mrs. Ira Nelson Morris, having been bought by her when her husband was ambassador to Japan and China in the 1920s.

OPEN: The Peabody Museum is open from 9 a.m. to 5 p.m. Mon.

through Sat., 1 to 5 p.m. on Sun. and holidays. Closed New Year's Day, Thanksgiving Day, and Christmas Day. One of the outstanding marine museums in the country.

ADMISSION TO MUSEUM: Adults, $1.00; children 6 to 15, 50¢; under 6, free.

ADDRESS: 161 Essex St., Salem, MA 01970. Telephone: 617-745-1876.

Left, bronze lantern in the Japanese garden at the Peabody Museum of Salem. (George Taloumis)

Michigan

Saginaw

Tokushima-Saginaw Friendship Garden

This Japanese garden grew out of Saginaw's Sister City relationship with the city of Tokushima in Japan. A people-to-people chapter was formed in 1960, which led to a continuing two-way exchange of visitors, gifts, ideas and understanding.

Funds for the creation of a Tokushima-Saginaw Friendship Garden were raised by this chapter. Yataro Suzue, a well-known landscape architect of Tokushima, generously gave of his time and talents as consultant in its construction.

The garden is almost an acre in size, with a narrow stream winding along past stone lanterns over a simple bridge, within earshot of a shallow waterfall. Near a large pond there is an *azumaya* (resting place) which welcomes visitors who wish to relax and enjoy the quiet scene. Large trees which antedate the garden's creation lend an air of permanence to this new symbol of friendship between peoples of two distant lands.

OPEN: Daily.

ADMISSION: Free.

ADDRESS: Ezra Rust Dr. at Washington Ave.

MAINTAINED BY: Saginaw Department of Parks and Recreation, 1574 S. Washington Ave., Saginaw, MI 48601. Telephone: 517-753-5411.

A brook in the Takushima-Saginaw Friendship Garden. (Saginaw Department of Parks and Recreation)

Minnesota

Minneapolis

The Japanese Garden at Radisson Inn Plymouth

"If you stand by the stone and gaze at it long enough, the stone will speak to you." That is one of the suggestions of landscape architect Shinichi Maesaki for viewing this Japanese "dry garden" which he designed in 1974. It is placed in the center of the Radisson Inn Plymouth complex, where it can be enjoyed by guests from windows or by walking along its stepping-stone path. The luxurious Japanese suite also has sliding doors from which overnight visitors may enter an equally Japanese atmosphere in the garden. The small souvenir folder which is given to the inn's guests explains that in strolling through, "one does not contemplate the garden with the eyes alone. One sees with the soul, hears with the heart, and perceives with the inner eye the calming, harmonious tranquility the Japanese call *yugen*." The path wends its way from a shallow "shore" past the raked sand representing moving water; along a "pond," and up to the vertical rocks simulating a waterfall. Graceful birches, dark yews, Japanese maples and carefully selected flowering shrubs soften the outlines. Surely visitors will do as suggested and let this quiet "stream" carry off jostling thoughts of the day!

The slogan of Radisson Inn Plymouth, owned jointly by companies in the United States and Japan, is that this is "Where East Meets West." The dark red and brown Tozai Restaurant building is designed like a Japanese farmhouse. Here diners are served in Japanese style. Though this is a very sophisticated modern hotel popular for conventions, it has an unusual, delightfully Oriental atmosphere. The beautiful Japanese garden is the focal point of the buildings—truly a place to relax and refresh the soul.

ADDRESS: Radisson Inn Plymouth, 2705 Annapolis Lane, Minneapolis, MN 55441. Telephone: 612-553-1600. (Plymouth is a

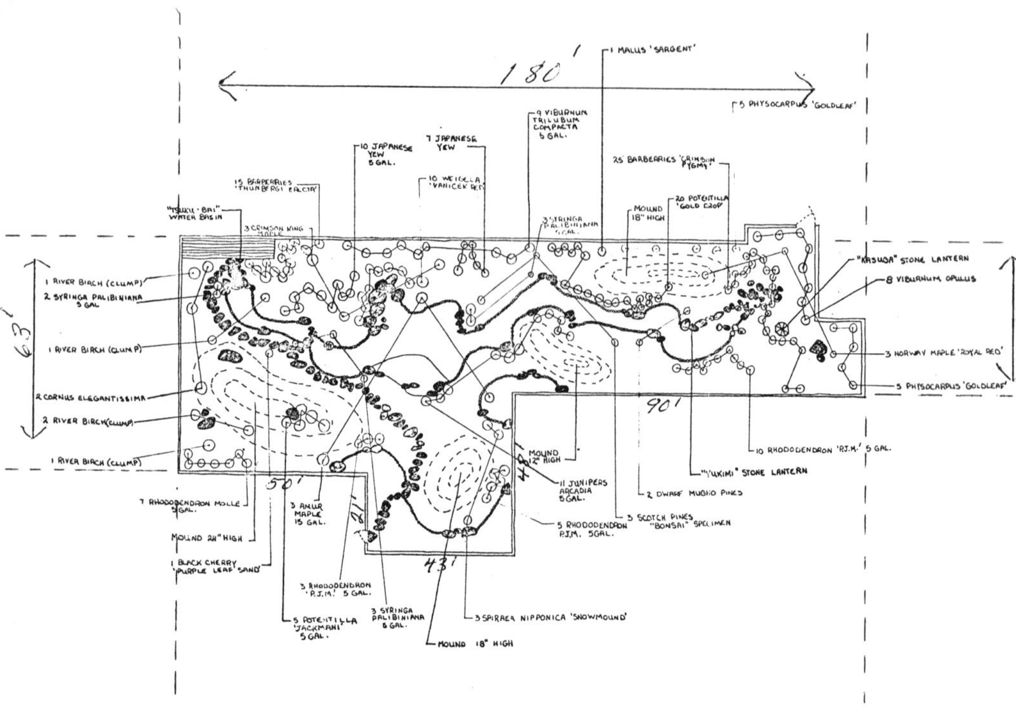

Above, plan of Minneapolis garden; right, statue of Kuan Yin, goddess of mercy at Mynelle Gardens. (Philip Colson)

suburb of Minneapolis.) The inn is at the intersection of I-494 and Highway 55.

Mississippi

Jackson

Oriental Garden in Mynelle Gardens

Visitors to these glorious gardens filled with brilliant flowers find the Oriental garden a peaceful interlude, inviting rest and relaxation. It was designed by Philip Colson, with quiet paths lined

The feathery ground-covers almost give the effect of a Japanese moss garden in Mynelle Gardens. (Philip Colson)

with *liriope* and other ground covers near several reflection pools. Lovely Oriental lanterns, some of stone, others of unpainted iron, may be seen there. A stone statue of Kuan Yin, Chinese goddess of mercy, sits brooding under the fine old trees beside the pond. Azaleas are kept sheared in the Japanese tradition. The interesting rocks—volcanic or meteorite—seem to have been there forever.

Mynelle Gardens were created by their owner, Mynelle Westbrook Hayward, over a period of fifty years. She and her husband

Hal—who was an iris and camellia expert—traveled widely gathering ideas and plants for these gardens. There is something in bloom all the year around. One of the unique gardens is a collection of old-fashioned roses descended from varieties known from 1696-1894.

OPEN: Daily from dawn to dusk the year around.

ADMISSION: Adults $1.00, children under 12 free if accompanied by an adult. Special group rates. Home open by appointment. Telephone: 601-922-4011.

ADDRESS: Mynelle Gardens, 4738 Clinton Blvd., Jackson, MS 39216.

Missouri

Centralia

Chance Gardens

Chance Gardens were started in 1936 as a hobby in the backyard of his home by the late A. Bishop Chance. (He was a pioneer manufacturer of electric utility equipment and founder of the A. B. Chance Company.) The gardens were designed by Maude Dawson Taylor, landscape architect of Kansas City. There are many Oriental overtones here, beginning with the large *torii* used as an entrance gate, and an open pergola-shelter. An interesting feature, reminiscent of the caves constructed in the early Chinese landscape gardens, is a rock grotto lined with specimens from various

Missouri caverns. There are two stone bridges with rough cedar railings crossing the little stream which pours down from the hillside. Many of the flowers blooming throughout the garden are of Oriental origin.

OPEN: Daily, to 9:30 p.m., May to Oct. Garden is illuminated at night.

ADMISSION: Free.

ADDRESS: East Singleton St. (in the 300 block), Centralia, MO 65240. Telephone: 314-682-5521.

DIRECTIONS: From M-22 go south on Allen St., to Singleton St., then go 4 blocks east.

Rocks and pool in the Chance Gardens. (A.B. Chance Co.)

St. Louis

Japanese Garden at Missouri Botanical Garden

The new Japanese garden is scheduled to be completed by the end of 1976 as an addition to the world-famous Missouri Botanical Garden (affectionately known also as "Shaw's Garden"). The first steps toward its creation were due to the efforts of the Japanese-American Citizens League of Greater St. Louis. Designed by Professor Koichi Kawana of UCLA, one of the leading Japanese landscape architects in this country, it will be a very extensive "stroll garden" of ten acres. The original lake has been enlarged to twice its size and contains four islands. One is the site of a teahouse, while another is covered with flowering plum trees. An *azumaya* (garden shelter) offers a place for the relaxation of visitors. Beyond is an overlook presenting a fine picture of the waterfall. The Yatsuhashi bridge, in zigzag style, crosses a beautiful planting of Japanese iris. The cost of another bridge—this one of logs edged with ground covers—was contributed by Chemtech Industries, Inc. A very fine imported *Kasuga* lantern is a memorial gift. The East Central District of the Federated Garden Clubs of Missouri made a special project of raising funds to plant one of the islands. This is a garden resulting from the warm interest and generosity of many citizens. It is appropriate that the *hiraniwa* or sand-and-stone garden, a quiet walled-in area for meditation, is adjacent to the headquarters of the National Council of State Garden Clubs.

Since the climate of central Japan is almost identical with that of St. Louis, many Japanese plants formerly unknown in this region could be included. These make the Japanese garden a splendid horticultural addition to the Botanical Garden. The needed color and form of rocks were not to be found locally and had to be imported from Colorado. Together with the black Japanese pines which have now been planted, they give the entire garden a truly authentic atmosphere of tranquil beauty.

OPEN: Missouri Botanical Garden is open from 9 a.m. to sundown, daily, except Christmas and New Year's Day.

ADMISSION: $1.00 for adults, 25¢ for children under 12, including the new Japanese garden when it is ready.

Rendering by Koichi Kawana, designer of the new Japanese garden at Missouri Botanical Garden, to show how part of it will look some day. (Photo by Missouri Botanical Garden)

ADDRESS: Missouri Botanical Garden, 2315 Tower Grove Ave., St. Louis, MO 63110. Telephone: 314-865-0440.

DIRECTIONS: Some special bus tours go to the garden; also the Bi-State bus lines, Sarah (42), Park-Southampton (80), and Lafayette (99).

New Jersey

Lakewood

Japanese Garden at Georgian Court College

This Japanese garden at Georgian Court College is a very old one, of beautiful design. It was laid out in the early part of this century on a one-acre part of the estate of George Gould. The garden was planned by the famous Japanese landscape architect, Takeo Shiota, who came to the United States in 1907 and is credited with designing the greatest number of Japanese gardens on the Atlantic seaboard. In 1923 the estate was acquired by Georgian Court College.

Entrance to the Japanese garden is through a hooded gateway. The path leads along and over a meandering brook, decorated on its banks with stone lanterns, rocks and beautiful old trees including some fine Japanese maples. The lovely teahouse is still intact. It is a peaceful spot, a quiet refuge for students and faculty.

OPEN: Weekdays, 10 a.m. to 5 p.m., throughout the year.

ADMISSION: Free.

ADDRESS: Georgian Court College, Lakewood, NJ 08701. Telephone: 201-364-2200.

The brook and stone lanterns in the Japanese garden at Georgian Court College. (Georgian Court College)

Somerville

*Chinese, Japanese and Indo-Persian Gardens at
Duke Gardens Foundation, Inc.*

Three Oriental gardens are among the eleven superb examples of traditional gardens of the world, created by Doris Duke in 1958. Each garden in this series of glass houses is perfect in detail, with every feature and plant authentic. They give a visitor an incredible feeling of space, even though some of the gardens are only 100 square feet in size.

The Japanese garden is subdued and subtle, in shades of gray, green and brown. The entrance is through a Japanese gate, opening onto a path past a small pool and over a little log bridge. Several stone lanterns are ready to furnish light, and a purification basin stands among low greenery.

The Chinese garden, designed by Richard C. Tongg, ASLA, is unique in America since it represents an authentic section of the traditional Chinese landscape garden. The "moon gate" entrance is set into a subtly decorated wall. Through it one sees the garden in a perfect framing. The stone path is paved in carefully designed irregularity, and bordered by a handsome open railing. This leads over a fine stone bridge and brook. Nearby are tall, dramatic rocks in groups, and a mysterious cave. The bulk of stone contrasts sharply with the feathery foliage of bamboo and willow trees and the delicate tracery of vines. The high curve of the bridge combines with its reflection into another moon-circle. One forgets the glass roof and walls entirely and feels as if one were in a great Chinese landscape leading endlessly on.

The Indo-Persian or *Mogul garden* is another outstanding reproduction which is not found anywhere else in our country. It has the authentic formality of two straight paths of geometric tiles, bordering a narrow central canal. On each side are borders of low, bright annuals set in precise rows. These are interrupted at intervals by closely clipped cypresses. Halfway along the paths on each side are cream-colored screens of delicate lacy design, giving the effect of the exquisite tracery in Indian and Persian temples. Passing beyond these, one comes to the central focal point: a short, shallow cascade of water flowing over tiers of small niches

The stone bridge, tall rocks and willow in the Chinese garden at Duke Gardens Foundation, Inc. (Dorothy Loa McFadden)

which hold candles. This delightful idea for viewing twinkling candlelight through a sheet of water, or reflected in a pool, was a favorite one in the gardens of old India.

There are other very beautiful gardens offered in this tour of unique greenhouses: French, English, Italian, desert, orchid jungle, and others—each a joy to behold.

OPEN: By advance reservation only (see address and telephone number below). Open 7 days a week from 1 to 5 p.m., Sept. through May, except Christmas and New Year's Day. Guides are provided and visitors are shown through in small groups on a tour lasting about an hour.

ADMISSION: (Paid at the Administration Building upon arrival): Adults $1.75 each, or in scheduled groups of 10 or more, $1.50 each. School groups of 15 children accompanied by two adults, free. Cameras and high-heeled shoes not allowed in the gardens.

ADDRESS: Duke Gardens Foundation, Inc., Rte. 206, Somerville, NJ 08876. Telephone: 201-722-3700.

DIRECTIONS: Watch for sign on Rte. 206, just south of Somerville.

The Indo-Persian garden at Easter time, in the greenhouse gardens of the Duke Gardens Foundation, Inc.

New York

Buffalo

Mirror Lake Japanese Garden

This Japanese garden, still under construction, is an outgrowth of Buffalo's Sister City relationship with Kanazawa in Japan. Ever since 1962, the two cities have exchanged students, art exhibits, gifts and visits by businessmen learning from each other. The Buffalo-Kanazawa Sister Cities Committee, sponsored by the Buffalo Area Chamber of Commerce, is the prime mover in this new garden project.

The financing and work for the Japanese garden has come from many other organizations and individuals as well. More than $150,000 worth of time, labor and materials have been donated by construction companies and other groups. These include the Rotary Club of Buffalo, the Western New York Nurserymen's Association, Ikebana International Chapter 50, and many other local clubs, all cooperating with the Maud Gordon Holmes Arboretum and the City Parks Department.

The first gift to the garden was from the Rotary Club of Buffalo: the planting of 100 Japanese cherry trees along the shore of Mirror Lake on the three-acre site allocated by the city. The original plans were drawn and donated by Roger Schneckenberger, local landscape architect, and then checked and approved by Mr. Komatsu of Kanazawa, a well-known garden designer there. Final dedication of the site for the Japanese garden came in the fall of 1974 in the presence of the mayor of Kanazawa.

Three small islands were created near the shore, connected to land by different types of bridges. The lantern, which is a central feature of Kanazawa's famous Kenroku-en Garden, was duplicated and sent by this sister city. Various other types of lanterns decorate the islands and paths along the water. Other gifts have included a *torii* gate, with a teahouse being planned for the future. Over 1000 plantings are underway, such as Japanese dogwood, creeping juniper, black and Austrian pine, and other evergreens. A pretty waterfall and resting places at special viewing points add beauty to this stroll garden along the lake. About twenty globe lanterns similar to those at the nearby state college light the garden at night, unifying it with the campus and casting their reflections in the water.

The spirit of friendship which underlies this Japanese garden project was well expressed by Buffalo's school superintendent, Dr. Joseph Manch, in a poem he wrote for one of the joint dedication ceremonies:

SALUTE TO KANAZAWA

How well we know that "hands across the sea"
Is not an idle phrase—that here and now
These words make meaning in this company
Of friends who come to share what hearts endow.
The space from shore to shore of our two lands
Is wide when measured by the sextant's sight—
But spirit knows no distance and our hands
Are clasped in deep affection, warm and tight.
And so our sister city beauty-blessed
We hail you, Kanazawa, as the place
Of virtue and delight in what is best
Of dignity and love of every race.
We take you to our hearts—and pray that we
May live with you in lasting unity.

OPEN: Daily.

ADMISSION: Free.

ADDRESS OF JAPANESE GARDEN: Delaware Park on Mirror Lake, near Elmwood Ave. exit of the expressway.

ADDRESS OF THE BUFFALO-KANAZAWA SISTER CITIES COMMITTEE: 238 Main St., Buffalo, NY 14202. Telephone: 716-852-5400.

Canandaigua

Japanese Garden in Sonnenberg Gardens

The Japanese garden here is one of nine very beautiful areas on the former estate of Mrs. Mary Clark Thompson, daughter of Myron H. Clark, once governor of the state of New York. She married Frederick Ferris Thompson, co-founder with his brother of the Chase Manhattan Bank of New York, who built the mansion at Sonnenberg in 1887. After her husband's death, Mrs. Thompson became interested in having the grounds laid out in a whole series of distinctive gardens, of which this Japanese garden is one. In the 1930s the estate became the property of the U.S. government which used the site for a veterans hospital. Fortunately the original fifty acres and house were left intact, and have now been restored by a unique cooperative effort of Canandaigua's citizens who have given generously since 1966 of their time, energy and money.

Below, the teahouse at Sonnenberg Gardens; overleaf, the bronze Buddha. (Photos by Sonnenberg Gardens)

The Japanese garden covers about four acres. It had been expertly designed by K. Vadamori, a renowned Japanese landscape architect, but, unfortunately, was damaged and vandalized more than any of the other gardens. However, since 1973 it has been recreated and is again admired for its exceptional beauty. The little brook running through it was planned in accordance with Japanese superstition to run from the east (source of purity) to the west (outlet for impurity). Each bridge is constructed differently—of logs, stone, earth or wooden surface. There is a pair of stone Foo Dogs, one smiling a welcome, the other scowling to ward off evil spirits. Among the other decorative features are a *torii* gate, a variety of lanterns, a stone pagoda, and a fine bronze Buddha. The teahouse, still being restored, is a replica of one which has since burned down in Kyoto, Japan. In front of the teahouse is the ritual purification basin. The trees and shrubs are mainly evergreens.

The other gardens consist of a patterned Italian parterre, a large rose garden, a blue and white English garden, a tiny fragrant "moonlight garden," a traditional Colonial garden, a rock garden, and a "secret garden."

OPEN: 9:30 a.m. to dusk, May through Oct.

ADMISSION: Adults $2.50, teens $1.00, children free. Tour of house included.

ADDRESS: Sonnenberg Gardens, 151 Charlotte St., Canandaigua, NY 14424. Telephone: 315-394-4922.

MAINTAINED BY: Sonnenberg Foundation from contributions.

DIRECTIONS: Canandaigua lies southeast of Rochester. Go 1½ miles northeast on State Rte. 332 to Ft. Hill Ave., right on to Charlotte St.

Millbrook

Innisfree Garden

This garden was named for the Irish "isle of peace" in Yeats' poem, "The Isle of Innisfree." It is a tranquil place, indeed, though designed with the Orient in mind rather than the Emerald Isle. It conforms with many of the basic principles of the ancient Chinese landscape gardens.

As early as 1895, artist Walter Beck began to study the pictorial quality of Eastern calligraphy and painting. Many of his finest pastels are in the Smithsonian in Washington, D.C., while his murals are much admired in Cincinnati's City Hall, the Art Museum in Brooklyn, N.Y., and the National Gallery in Washington. As his paintings became more and more influenced by Oriental art, so also did his creation of garden pictures on the 1000 acres surrounding his house. Over a period of twenty-two years, he brought the mountains, streams, and waterfalls into a series of beautiful pictures. He used rocks and plants, colors and form, in creating apparently natural garden scenes, just as he would use paints for his canvases.

One hillside is a glory of dogwoods; a stream is bordered with Japanese *primulas*; iris, forget-me-nots, and pink mallows add color just where he felt they were needed. There are constant surprises just as there were in the old Chinese gardens: a white garden of moss phlox, followed by white lotus, later white mallows; a startling and dramatic arrangement of rocks, topped by an Oriental lion-dog sculpture; then a peaceful scene of the fifty-acre lake with its water lilies and trees of varied textures placed for the best reflections. Wooden bridges lead to thatch-roofed shelters for peaceful contemplation. Although many of the trees were imported from the Orient and Europe, they all seem to have been there forever, bordering the patches of wildflowers and giving interesting variety of form and textures against the sky.

Mr. Beck died at the age of 90. In 1955 his widow willed the entire estate to the Innisfree Foundation, a nonprofit organization dedicated to the study of the Eastern and Western civilizations which have influenced garden art. What a legacy of natural Oriental beauty this fine painter left here for everyone to enjoy!

OPEN: May through Oct., Wed. through Fri. 10 a.m. to 4 p.m.; Sat. and Sun. 11 a.m. to 5 p.m. Closed Mon. and Tues. Open Mon. if a legal holiday.

ADMISSION: Free Wed. through Fri.; $1.00 for 16 years and older on Sat. and Sun. Admission includes viewing the gallery of

(Photos by Innisfree Gardens)

Mr. Beck's paintings and the home.

ADDRESS: Innisfree Garden, Tyrrel Rd., Millbrook, NY 12545. Telephone: 914-677-8000.

DIRECTIONS: Millbrook is about 85 miles north of New York City, 1¾ miles from the Taconic Parkway overpass on Rte. 44, turn right on Tyrrel Rd.

New York City (Brooklyn)

Three Japanese Gardens in Brooklyn Botanic Gardens

Three different types of Japanese gardens are included in the fifty acres of beautiful displays at Brooklyn Botanic Gardens: a Hill-and-Pond Garden; a Ryoanji Temple Stone Garden; and a Roji (dewy path to teahouse) Garden.

The large Hill-and-Pond Garden was designed in 1915 by the renowned Japanese landscape architect, Takeo Shiota, and was considered by many to be his masterpiece. It was a gift from the late Alfred T. White. The two-acre garden centers upon a small lake shaped like the Chinese character for "heart, soul, spirit." Standing in the water is a fine *torii* inscribed with the Japanese words *dai myo jin* ("great illuminating deity"), showing that it is dedicated to the Shinto god of the harvest. The "harvest shrine" which this refers to stands on a promontory nearby.

The viewing platforms and the adjacent "waiting house," usual outside of ceremonial teahouses, are planned not only for rest but also for enjoying the best views of the lake. On the shores there are weeping cherry trees, azaleas, Japanese iris, many fine pine trees, and pruned shrubs. Across the lake a small five-tiered cascade flows over "echo-caverns" to intensify the sound. Among the stone lanterns is a tall pagoda-type bearing the signs of the zodiac.

The Ryoanji Temple Stone Garden, opened to the public in 1963, is an exact recreation of the 500-year-old Ryoanji Garden at a temple in Kyoto. On a bed of finely crushed stone, raked to represent ripples on the sea, are fifteen rocks brought from Japan, arranged in groups of seven, five and three. They express the harmony underlying the universe. Visitors study the stone garden

Upper left, the drum bridge in the hill-and-pond garden; upper right, the purification basin; below, the lake and flowering cherries. (Brooklyn Botanic Garden)

Meditation at the Ryoanji Temple Stone Garden. (Brooklyn Botanic Garden)

from a long roofed platform after entering a beautiful Japanese gate. The garden was built under the supervision of Mr. Takuma P. Tono, landscape architect from Tokyo, and is unique as the only perfect copy of Japan's masterpiece of Zen meditation gardens in America.

The Roji Garden, meaning the "dewy path to the ceremonial teahouse," is the third and most recent garden here. It is small, 150 by 30 feet; designed by Mrs. Polly Fairman, landscape architect of Princeton, N.J., it was opened to the public in 1973. This type of garden originated in Japan in the sixteenth century during the time of the famous tea master, Rikyu. It is planned to simulate a bit of remote mountain wilderness, with delightful plantings of ferns and mosses which thrive under moist or dewy conditions.

Another form of Japanese garden art, that of growing bonsai (dwarf potted trees), is on display in the greenhouses here. Many are 50 to 100 years old, yet are less than two feet high, some merely inches tall. Brooklyn Botanic Gardens are certainly a mecca for all who love and want to study the various types of

Japanese gardens and to make a tour of horticultural Japan in one day.

OPEN: The Hill-and-Pond Garden is open from mid-April through Oct., 10:30 a.m. to 4 p.m. The Ryoanji Temple Stone Garden and Roji Garden may be seen May to Oct., 11 a.m. to 1 p.m., and 2 to 4 p.m.

ADMISSION: The Hill-and-Pond Garden is free on weekdays, 10¢ on weekends. The Ryoanji Temple Stone Garden and Roji Garden together, 25¢.

ADDRESS: Brooklyn Botanic Gardens, 1000 Washington Ave., Brooklyn, NY 11225. Telephone: 212-622-4433.

DIRECTIONS: Take 7th Ave. subway IRT Express downtown to Brooklyn Museum-Eastern Parkway Station; or BMT Brighton Line to Prospect Park Station.

North Salem

Stroll Garden of the Hammond Museum

This peaceful stroll garden was designed and planted 1959 by Natalie Hays Hammond after a visit to Japan. It includes a Zen garden for inward meditation, a dry landscape garden, and a Japanese teahouse. On an island in the pond stands a statue of Jizo, Japanese patron saint of children. The five water lilies in the reflecting pool are said to represent the attributes of Buddha: humanity, justice, courtesy, wisdom and fidelity. A recent addition is a parterre garden of the *I Ching*, its three symbols represented by lines of yellow sedum: companionship, peace and light.

One needs to read and follow the guide pamphlet, however, to understand the underlying Japanese philosophies of each section on these 3½ acres; for otherwise the gardens look simply like a pretty rural American scene and not at all like the traditional Japanese gardens.

OPEN: 11 a.m. to 5 p.m. Wed. through Sun. from May 30 through

Oct. (The museum is open to December 24th, with changing exhibits.)

ADMISSION: $1.00 for adults, to garden—$1.00 extra to museum; children 75¢ to garden—75¢ extra to museum. Japanese tea and refreshments are served in the teahouse from 2 to 4 p.m.

ADDRESS: Hammond Museum, Deveau Rd., North Salem, NY 10560. Telephone: 914-669-5033.

DIRECTIONS: From New York City, take Saw Mill River Parkway, go east on Rte. 116, then north a short distance on Rte. 124 to Deveau Rd. Go east on Deveau Rd. (Coming from Rte. 84, take exit 19 south.)

Ohio

Akron

Japanese Garden at Stan Hywet Hall

Stan Hywet Hall (pronounced *stan-hee-wet*, meaning "stone quarry" in Anglo-Saxon) is a former seventy-acre estate now open to the public. It was the home of F. A. Seiberling, founder of Goodyear and Seiberling Rubber Companies. The superb sixty-five-room Tudor manor house was built in 1911-15, and the original Japanese garden was also laid out then. Unfortunately, it fell into ruin during the depression years of the 1920s. In 1956, after Mr. Seiberling's death, his six children formed a foundation to operate Stan Hywet Hall as a museum and cultural center. The other gardens were then gradually restored, but the Japanese garden remained neglected.

The Kasuga lantern at night in the Japanese garden at Stan Hywet Hall. (General Electric Company, Cleveland)

Finally, in 1972, the Akron Men's Garden Club volunteered to reclaim the original beauty of this garden. With the aid of a well-known landscape architect, Kaneji Domoto of New Rochelle, New York, they reconstructed a portion of it. One of the foundation's board members, Mr. L. E. Judd, was so inspired on seeing the reconstruction that he offered to finance the rest of the work needed. Volunteers under Mr. Domoto's supervision completed the Japanese garden during the next year.

The fine old trees were well pruned, waterways and waterfalls were put in order, and rocks and donated stone lanterns were properly placed. Six varieties of moss were planted in the garden, and ferns, ground covers and azaleas soon grew as if they had always been there. The final exciting touch was added when experts from the General Electric Company were brought in to plan carefully designed night lighting. Soon evening visitors to Stan Hywet Hall could enjoy the garden's bright forms and shadowy silhouettes, and the dramatically lighted tree trunks.

Dramatic night lighting in the Japanese garden at Stan Hywet Hall. (Walter Long)

The great manor house here is considered by many to be the finest example of Tudor architecture in America. It is filled with priceless furniture and art treasures. The grounds deserve a separate visit by garden lovers, as they include several formal gardens. Among these are the English Garden, the Rose Garden, and the Perennial Garden. In addition there are extensive specialized areas for thousands of peonies, tulips, irises, day lilies, and chrysanthemums. The English Garden is also illuminated at night.

OPEN: 10 a.m. to 4:15 p.m. every weekday except Mon.; 1-5 p.m. Sun. The Japanese garden is open from June through Oct. 15; the other gardens from early May through Oct. 15.

ADMISSION: Tours of house and garden—adults, $2.50; children 6 to 12, $1.00; under 6, free. Group rates available. Garden tours only—$1.25 for adults; 50¢ for children. Tours of the house last one hour. Visitors may wander through the grounds on their own. Art shows, music festivals, garden marts, and the annual "Wonderful World of Ohio Mart" are among the many events taking place here. There is also a picnic area and gift shop.

ADDRESS: Stan Hywet Hall Foundation, Inc., 714 N. Portage Path, Akron, OH 44303. Telephone: 216-836-5533.

DIRECTIONS: From Ohio Turnpike take exits 11 or 12 by I-77 or State Rte. 8. Easy access from all major routes.

Cleveland

City of Cleveland Japanese Garden

This Japanese garden is a charming, quiet place, popular with visitors to Cleveland's Rockefeller Park Greenhouses. It was designed by John G. Michalko, city commissioner of shade trees, and has an area of 4000 square feet.

The paths of river-bottom stone wind along to a small waterfall. The pool may be crossed on stepping stones, and there is a stone water basin. A number of stone benches are placed at convenient intervals. (This attractive feature, unfortunately, is missing in many Japanese gardens.) Here visitors can sit quietly to absorb the beauty of the Japanese maples, bamboos, azaleas, rhododendrons, and a metasequoia. One of these seats is made from an old millstone. The two entrances have the traditional small bamboo-covered roofs.

This Japanese garden is just north of the formal entrance to the Rockefeller Park Greenhouses where garden lovers may also enjoy a tropical palm house, flower displays which are changed each season, and sections for ferns, cacti and 1000 orchids. Next to these is the "Talking Garden for the Blind."

OPEN: Daily, 8 a.m. to 4:30 p.m.

ADMISSION: Free.

ADDRESS: 750 East 88th St., Cleveland, OH 44108. Greenhouse telephone: 216-694-3103. Park Commissioner at City Hall: 216-694-2490.

Cleveland

The Japanese Garden at the Garden Center of Greater Cleveland

This new Japanese garden was dedicated on May 20, 1975, at a ceremony attended by the Honorable Masao Kanazawa, Deputy Permanent Representative of Japan to the United Nations, and Madame Kanazawa. It was a joyful occasion marking the culmination of ten years of devoted planning and hard work by the members of Cleveland's Chapter 20 of Ikebana International. These dedicated women surveyed the possible sites, made the selection, and chose the designer, Mr. David A. Slawson, who had studied the art of Japanese garden design in Japan under the noted expert, Professor Kinsaku Nakane. Their enthusiasm aroused the interest of city officials who donated the land, and the cooperation and gifts from six other garden clubs in Cleveland, the Cleveland Horticultural Society, and many private contributors, thus making the garden possible.

The site of the Japanese garden lies between the Garden Center's lower lawn and a wooded ravine, an area of 90 by 120 feet. A fine specimen of dawn redwood was already there, and tons of boulders which had to be removed from the hillside were utilized

Above, the dry cascade; below, the purification basin. (Steven A. Frowine)

for the stairs and for accents in the plan. The visitor sees the garden first by descending a few steps and looking through a framing of trellis covered with wisteria. The near part of this scene is a dry, Zen-type garden with rocks representing a cascading mountain waterfall apparently continuing as a stream lined with a stony beach. Low profile shrubs such as evergreens, azaleas, taxus, Japanese holly, Pygmy barberry and dwarf Mugho pine soften the hillside and the edges of the rocky "stream," while Japanese maples add color among the evergreens. A tall stone pagoda gleams against the hill. A path of stepping stones leads one across the lawn to the dry cascade and small stone bridge. Beyond that is just the suggestion of a tea garden area, with a stone water basin and lantern. It is an interesting design combining these two forms of traditional Japanese garden—the dry Zen garden and the tea garden.

OPEN: Mon. through Fri., 9 a.m. to 5 p.m.; Sun., 2 to 5 p.m.

ADMISSION: Free.

ADDRESS: 11030 East Blvd., Cleveland, OH 44106. Telephone: 216-721-1600.

MAINTAINED BY: Ikebana International. Cleveland Chapter 20 has set up a tax-exempt Maintenance/Endowment Fund for contributions to take care of the garden.

Newark

Japanese Garden at Dawes Arboretum

The designer of this garden, Mr. Makoto Nakamura, thought of it as an exchange of two cultures—American and Japanese—rather than as an authentically traditional Japanese garden. Although it adheres to the Japanese idea of suggesting rather than copying natural scenery, he felt that in these surroundings in Ohio the motif was strictly American. Mr. Nakamura was lecturer in landscape architecture at the University in Kyoto when he came to America in 1964. This was under a cultural exchange agreement, between his university and the U.S. Department of State, to spend eight months at Dawes Arboretum in planning this garden.

Entrance to the Japanese garden is through a windbreak of dark spruce which makes a background for groves of flowering cherries. The surrounding rugged boulders and a "dry stream" were planned to represent a forceful American landscape. Emerging from this woodland, one comes to a garden of typical Japanese elements: a lake, islands connected by bridges, shoreline rock compositions, and a pebbly beach. The paths lead gradually to a simple meditation house. Benches are placed at strategic points where visitors may rest and enjoy particularly lovely views.

Many of the plantings are native to Japan: kerria, Japanese yew, flowering quince, Japanese maple, and others. Because of the severe climate of Ohio, however, European and American plants had to be used also, such as rhododendrons, dogwoods, and various evergreen trees.

The 3½ acres devoted to this serene Japanese garden are only a part of Dawes Arboretum, which has a splendid collection of some 2000 species of trees and shrubs on its 950 acres.

Shoreline of the lake. (George S. Rosenthal)

OPEN: During daylight hours, throughout the year. Exhibit of dwarf bonsai trees in Administration Building. Guided tours. Two picnic areas.

ADMISSION: Free.

ADDRESS: Dawes Arboretum, Rte. 5, Box 270, Newark, OH 43055. Telephone: 614-323-2355; or 614-323-2990.

DIRECTIONS: Go 5 miles south of Newark on State Rte. 13.

Oberlin

Japanese Garden at Oberlin College

A very beautiful Japanese garden was created in 1964 outside of the Conservatory of Music at Oberlin College. It is about 65 by 100 feet, located against the building so that passersby on the

Japanese garden at Oberlin. (Jack Sterling)

sidewalk can enjoy it at any time of day, and also at night when it is dramatically illuminated. Students within the conservatory building can also see it since one section projects slightly into the garden, thus allowing a fine view through two windows.

The conservatory was designed by Japanese architect Minoru Yamasaki, who also gave final approval to the plans for the garden as drawn by Eichstedt and Griffin Associates of Grosse Pointe, Michigan. It was on the shores of the lake at Oberlin College that they found the greatest attraction for the garden: two old pine trees which had been bent and twisted by the winds in a way to bring joy to the heart of any Japanese garden designer. The weathered stones were imported from Indiana. Low Mugho pines complete the restful picture—a quiet oasis on the busy campus, lovely under the snows of winter as well as throughout the rest of the year.

ADDRESS: Corner of West College St. and South Professor St.

FOR FURTHER INFORMATION: Phone 216-775-8121, or write Oberlin College, Oberlin, OH 44074.

Oklahoma

Grove

Satsuki Gardens

Satsuki Gardens were named for the many azaleas of the Satsuki variety planted here. This is a charming Japanese garden designed by Dr. Leonard O. Miller next to his dental office. It was opened in March 1975 for the enjoyment of his fellow citizens in this small town (population 1000).

The garden's entrance is a wooden *torii* gate. A stream runs into a reflection pool where it is crossed by an arched bridge. Most of the plants are evergreens, with rhododendrons (rare in Oklahoma) as a background, thus keeping to the Japanese tradition of a year-round green garden. In spring the Satsuki and Kurume azaleas add bright color. Paths wind around under the oak trees beside an occasional stone Japanese lantern.

OPEN: Daily.

ADMISSION: Free.

ADDRESS: 2201 South Main St., Grove, OK 74344. Mail: P.O. Box 672.

DIRECTIONS: Grove is in the northeast corner of Oklahoma; northeast of Tulsa, via highway #69 (22 miles east of Vinita).

Oregon

Portland

Japanese Garden

Surely this is one of the most beautiful Japanese gardens in America, serene and varied in all four seasons!

In 1959, Portland established a Sister City relationship with the Japanese city of Sapporo in the district of Hokkaido, which has a very similar climate and type of flora. When the Japan-America Conference of Mayors and Chamber of Commerce Presidents met in Portland in 1961, delegates came to the site of the present Japanese garden for dedication ceremonies, and planted camellia bushes received from nineteen cities of Japan. The following year

The gate behind the moss garden. (Terry Bieritz)

Above left, the Haiku Poetry Stone; right, the Nure Sagi lantern; below left, the zigzag bridge. (Photos by Terry Bieritz) Below right, the ornamental stone pagoda. (A.L. Tompkins)

the Japanese Garden Society of Oregon was incorporated, and began raising funds to create the new garden. Although there has been splendid cooperation from city officials and the Park Bureau, there has never been any tax money appropriated for this 5½ acre Japanese garden.

In 1963, the Japanese Garden Society of Oregon retained Professor Takuma P. Tono to design and supervise their garden. Professor Tono is a graduate of Hokkaido University in Sapporo, holds a degree in landscape architecture from Cornell, and was formerly head of the Landscape Architecture Department of Tokyo Agricultural University. He agreed that the site was a perfect one, especially as it has a beautiful natural forest background and overlooks majestic Mount Hood—now included as "borrowed scenery" so dear to Japanese garden designers—an Oregon version of Mount Fuji.

Actually this is a series of five traditional gardens. To the left of the entrance gate is the *flat garden*, one of the earliest Japanese landscape forms. Its design, so true to those at a few ancient temples in Japan, is rarely seen in America. Besides combining sand, mossy rocks and a very few trees and shrubs, its main points of interest are the "island" plantings of tiny ruby dianthus in two shapes: the circle in the form of a sake cup, the other a gourd or sake bottle, both denoting pleasure. (A deeper philosophical meaning is that the circle symbolizes enlightenment and perfection, and the gourd denotes happiness.) The large bluish-green stone in this garden came from the island of Shikoku. The surrounding sand is raked in patterns to represent the sea. Nearby is a black upright Haiku poetry stone, a delightful innovation. The Japanese characters inscribed on it in seventeen white syllables may be roughly translated: "Here I saw the same soft spring as in Japan."

Behind the flat garden is a small pond and the *moss garden*—one of the most beautiful forms of Japanese garden, rare in America. The many varieties of mosses and ferns catching the sunlight make this another spot of great tranquility. Nearby is a wisteria arbor carefully placed to frame a view of the five-story pagoda lantern, a gift from Sapporo.

At one side is the *sand-and-stone garden*, its abstract forms expressing the symbolism and mystery of Zen. In this case, however, there is an added meaning from an old Japanese legend. It was said that a tigress cast her seven cubs into the sea to test their courage, but they began to starve. Then Buddha, taking pity on them, plunged in and offered himself as food. He is represented by the tall stone in the "sea" of sand, while the other rocks represent the baby tigers.

The *strolling pond garden* centers around two pools. These are connected by a stream which is lined with fifty varieties of Japanese iris—a breathtaking sight, reminiscent of the Iris Garden at Meiji Shrine in Tokyo. The path around the ponds is so designed that new views and features appear at every turn. The cascading Heavenly Falls add a musical accompaniment. From the bridge crossing the stream a most interesting stone lantern can be seen, called the *nure sagi.* Its tall, stooped shape is said to resemble a heron with wet feathers, feeling lonesome in the rain. Another lantern standing on two long legs is a *kotoji doro* or "harp tuner," supposed to resemble the tuning fork used for the Japanese musical instrument, the koto.

The *tea garden*, a traditional *roji-niva* or "dewy path" garden, is attached to the ceremonial teahouse. Entrance is through a charming small bamboo gate. The building was first constructed in Japan using only pegs, no nails, then reassembled here. The sliding *shoji* paneled walls are planned to open a special view of the garden, however they are stationed. In front is a stone lantern to light the low water basin. At its left is a *teshoku-seki* stone ("to rest a candlestick on") and on the right, a *yuto-seki* stone ("to place a pail on") with another flat rock in front on which a person can stand or kneel. The teahouse is not used except as a typical example of this kind of building.

The Japanese Garden Society of Oregon can certainly be proud of these beautiful gardens. The plantings have been done to assure beauty and subtle variations of color throughout the spring, summer and autumn. Still in the planning stage is a large main pavilion with a viewing terrace overlooking the city and the panorama beyond, including glorious Mt. Hood.

OPEN: April 1 to Memorial Day, Tues. to Fri., 10 a.m. to 4 p.m.; Sat. and Sun., noon to 6 p.m. Shuttle-bus on weekends only. Memorial Day through Labor Day, Tues. to Sat., 10 a.m. to 6 p.m.; Sun., 10 a.m. to 8 p.m. Shuttle-bus daily. Labor Day through

The traditional flat garden, featuring beds of tiny ruby dianthus shaped like a sake cup and a gourd – symbols of happiness. (Terry Bieritz)

Oct., Tues. to Fri., 10 a.m. to 4 p.m.; Sat. and Sun., noon to 6 p.m., shuttle-bus on weekends only. Open National Holiday Mondays, 10 a.m. to 6 p.m.

ADMISSION: Adults $1.00, children under 6 free. Students, senior citizens and military personnel, 50¢. Group rates and guide service must be arranged in advance. No charge for shuttle-bus from parking lot to garden.

MAILING ADDRESS: The Japanese Garden Society of Oregon, P.O. Box 3847, Portland, OR 97208. Telephone: 503-223-1321, or 503-223-4070.

SPECIAL EVENTS: During May, Carp Kites are flown to celebrate Japan's Boys' Day. On Mothers' Day there is a bonsai exhibition. In late June, when the Japanese iris is in bloom, there is an Ikebana-Iris Display at the teahouse. A Japanese Star Festival is held during July featuring Japanese folk dancers. On certain days in August, Japanese models wearing kimonos will pose for photographers in the garden.

DIRECTIONS: The Japanese garden is located on S.W. Kingston Ave., directly above the International Rose Test Garden in Washington Park, in Portland's West Hills Section.

Pennsylvania

Bethlehem

Serenity Garden

The creation of this Serenity Garden is an inspiring story of Japanese friendship and generosity. It all began with a warm Sister City relationship between Bethlehem, often called the "Christmas City" of America, and Tondabayashi (near Osaka in Japan), which has a large Christmas ornament industry. In 1960 this people-to-people goodwill idea was fostered by the Reverend Kenneth Heim, a former Bethlehem pastor transferred to Japan. Soon many travelers from Bethlehem. began visiting Tondabayashi. One of these was Lawrence Fenninger, vice-president of Bethlehem Steel Company, who greatly admired the garden in Tondabayashi's city center and commented that he wished Bethlehem had something like it. To his amazement, landscape architect Yoshinaga Sakon immediately offered to go to Bethlehem at his own expense and design a garden there. Sakon, who was well-known as a Japanese garden expert, had laid out part of Japan's Expo '70 garden and a large garden for the Osaka Royal Hotel.

In September 1970 Mr. Sakon arrived in Bethlehem, looked over the available site at the city center, and immediately got to work. Within ten days he and his two assistants had scoured the countryside for suitable rocks and supervised the construction by city workmen of a small waterfall, a pond and a bridge, and decided on the future plantings. As a gesture of gratitude, the city renamed the area Sakon Plaza. Serenity Garden was dedicated in May 1971 with Mr. Sakon, United Nations Japanese Ambassador Nobuhiko Ushiba, and local dignitaries taking part.

Later, in 1974, Mr. Sakon decided to give Bethlehem a traditional Japanese teahouse for the garden. He had it prefabricated in Tondabayashi, then taken apart for shipment, and accompanied workmen to Bethlehem to set it up there. For some time afterward there was an impasse in finding the money in Bethlehem for a copper roof since neither the parks department nor the city itself had the needed $4700. The teahouse looked drab under a covering of tar paper. However, when the citizens began a drive for donations, two companies offered to contribute the needed materials and labor. Since Lehigh Engineering had the preferred copper, their offer was gratefully accepted, plant laborers contributed their time, the splendid roof was finished, and the Serenity Garden was ready for a visit from Mayor Nishioka of Tondabayashi. His city, meanwhile, had arranged a "Bethlehem Room" in its city hall.

The creation of this lovely garden is certainly an inspiring story of Japanese generosity and friendship. It all started from Bethlehem's Sister City relationship and the work of its dedicated Sister City Commission.

OPEN: Daylight hours. Tour provided upon request.

ADMISSION: Free.

ADDRESS: Sakon Plaza, City Center Complex. Address for information: Bethlehem Parks Department, 10 E. Church St., Bethlehem, PA 18018. Telephone: 215-865-7079.

The Garden of Serenity. (Bethlehem Steel Corporation)

Malvern

Gardens of Japan at Swiss Pines

These Japanese gardens covering fifteen acres are a joy to explore. When Mr. Arnold Bartschi, a Swiss shoe manufacturer, first bought the house and grounds in 1957, he discovered some Oriental statuary hidden in the overgrown shrubs. These inspired him with the idea of creating a Japanese garden. For his first "five-year plan" he engaged the well-known New York landscape architect, David H. Engel, a specialist in Japanese garden art. During the following five years, the garden was enlarged still more under the direction of Japanese architect Katsuo Saito, with Mr. Bartschi himself very much involved throughout.

There are two different stone-and-gravel Zen gardens for meditation, with rake marks representing waves of the sea. All the other areas are of the hill-and-pond stroll garden type, through which the paths wander casually, uncovering new vistas and ornamental features at each turn. These include some seventy statues and lanterns, but in this large garden they are so carefully placed that there is not the slightest sense of crowding. Each pond or pool has a different type of simple bridge, one being covered with an open trellis. The large peaceful Buddha statue, the five-story stone pagoda, the mysterious little path through a bamboo grove—each presents a different picture for quiet contemplation. The teahouse, a copy of a very old one in Japan, is approached through the traditional serene garden path. At another point a tiny open-sided resting pavilion invites the visitor to pause again.

The trees and shrubs have been kept clipped in Japanese fashion, but throughout the gardens mountain laurel, rhododendrons, azaleas, flowering crabs and dogwoods bloom in season. There are beautiful carpets of moss under the trees, as well as luxuriant ground covers.

If the visitor has not had his fill while strolling through these serene Japanese gardens, he may want to search out the various others as well—the rose garden, the heather area, the wildflower trail, and Mr. Bartschi's special joy and pride: the herb garden with separate beds for those herbs with culinary uses, and others for aromatic fragrance.

(Swiss Pines)

Above, the latticed bridge; below, one of the Zen Meditation gardens. (Swiss Pines)

OPEN: 10 a.m. to 4 p.m. weekdays. Saturdays from 9 a.m. to noon, Mar. 15 to Dec. 15. Guided tours for groups up to 20 can be arranged for a fee. Closed on holidays.

ADMISSION: Free.

ADDRESS: Swiss Pines, Charlestown Rd., R.D. 1, Malvern, PA 19355. Telephone: 215-933-6916.

MAINTAINED BY: The Bartschi Foundation, associated with the Academy of Natural Sciences of Philadelphia.

DIRECTIONS: From Lincoln Highway in Malvern (Rte. 30) turn at light onto Rte. 29. Pass under Pa. Turnpike overpass for about 200 ft.; continue straight ahead on Charlestown Rd. to Swiss Pines. Or, from Phoenixville: coming through town on Nutt Rd., turn at light at Fountain Inn on Bridge Rd. which becomes Charlestown Rd., to Swiss Pines.

Philadelphia

Japanese Exhibition House and Garden

The Japanese Exhibition House was made in Nagoya, Japan, in 1953. It was sent to the Museum of Modern Art in New York as a gift from the American-Japan Society of Japan to the people of the United States. The design by the noted architect Junzo Yoshimura is in the style of a sixteenth- or seventeenth-century home of a scholar, government official or priest. As was the custom in Japan, the outer sliding paper walls (*shoji*) of the main rooms could be pushed aside so that the occupants, sitting on cushions on the floor, could enjoy a view of the garden. The veranda runs around three sides of the house and was also used for looking out over the planted area and pond. Thus the garden was designed to be seen from the inside of the house as is usual in homes of Japan today (a different concept from the stroll gardens in more public areas, as shown in many examples in this book).

The Exhibition House was moved to Fairmount Park in Philadelphia in 1957, and there the Japanese landscape designer Tansai Sano, with David H. Engel as consultant, laid out the garden. There is quite a large lake filled with lotus and water lilies to be

The Japanese Exhibition House in the Fairmount Park. (Dr. Raymond R. Lapelle)

seen from the house. This is fed by a small stream, which runs under the bridge connecting the house with the ceremonial tea-house and bath. Symbolically, the stream represents a river, running into the "ocean" which is the pond. Dwarf bamboo and pine take the place of a forest. The rocks, brought from Nagoya, are upright, pointing to heaven to indicate a temple, while others in the water represent the islands of Japan. There is a small waterfall pouring into the pond, and a five-tiered stone pagoda ornaments the shoreline.

It is sad to relate that in this wonderful old city which was the site of the first Japanese garden in America (at the Centennial International Exhibition of 1876), the Exhibition House and garden are now neglected and unkempt. Recently they have even been badly vandalized. It is to be hoped that Philadelphia's city officials and citizens will awaken to their responsibility and restore this beautiful historic place, with all its educational values and story of international generosity and goodwill.

OPEN: We hope it soon will be. Information should be sought

from the Fairmount Park Commission, Memorial Hall West Park, Philadelphia, PA 19131. Telephone: 215-686-1776.

ADDRESS (of House and Garden): West Fairmount Park, Lansdowne Dr., at Belmont Ave., Philadelphia.

Rhode Island

Providence

Two Japanese Gardens in Roger Williams Park

It is unusual for a public park in one of our great cities to have two Japanese gardens, but here they are. The first one, created in 1965, covers about 1½ acres, and is a hilly stroll garden. The visitor is greeted by an eight-foot lantern at the main entrance—a beautiful gate in the surrounding redwood fence. Boulders and hills create a serene landscape through which the paths wind their way to a teahouse. Curved wooden bridges cross over the stream. Beeches and flowering cherries can be found there, and black pines have been sculptured to suit the garden.

The second Japanese garden was designed in 1973 by Oronzo Vescera, after several visits to Japan. Mr. Vescera was born in Italy, but seems to have a particular affinity for the art of Japanese gardening. He has won recognition with his bonsai displays from the Rhode Island Federation of Garden Clubs. As horticulture supervisor for the nursery division of the city park department, he not only planned the new Japanese garden but is responsible for the planting and pruning done there. This is a dry garden of the hill type, laid out on a 40 by 150 foot plot beside the Charles H. Smith Memorial Greenhouse. Here zigzag bridges of different heights span the rocks giving the illusion of dry rivers.

Cryptomeria trees and hemlocks provide a forest background, with lower shrubs, including mountain laurel and a few azaleas, bordering the "stream." One part of this garden is of the Zen meditation type, with a "sea" of raked gravel surrounding "islands" of rock.

OPEN: The earlier garden is open daily; the more recent one, from 10:30 a.m. to 4 p.m.

ADMISSION: Free.

ADDRESS: Roger Williams Park, Elmwood Ave., Providence, RI 02905.

South Carolina

Sumpter

Swan Lake Iris Gardens

Though Swan Lake Iris Gardens are not Oriental in design, we have included them because of the thousands of Japanese iris which thrive so well in the black swampy soil there. Seeing these in bloom in May and June is a sight never to be forgotten. It is reminiscent of the spectacular iris gardens at the Meiji Shrine in Tokyo, Japan, to which many thousands of Japanese make a pilgrimage each year in the spring. Truly, this exquisite flower, native to the Land of the Rising Sun, has found an appropriate setting in America in the quiet natural beauty of these gardens.

They were started originally in 1927 by Mr. H. C. Bland on his own land. Then he took over adjoining property given to the city by Mr. A. T. Heath, and made the combination more beautiful each year. Finally the entire gardens were dedicated as the property of the city Parks and Recreation Department in 1956.

These 120 acres of lawns, flower gardens, lake and pinewoods have become a national and international attraction. There is something in bloom from March to November. The black swamp water of the lake reflects some fifty swans as they glide about—white swans from England, black swans from Australia. Water lilies of all colors cover much of the lake, while the exotic Egyptian lotus blooms nearer the shore where ancient cypresses droop over them. Wandering along the paths one crosses rustic bridges to pretty islands, and inhales the fragrance of the many blossoming trees and shrubs.

OPEN: Daily, 7 a.m. to 7 p.m. Picnic area.

ADMISSION: Free.

ADDRESS: Swan Lake Iris Gardens, West Liberty St., Sumter, SC 29150. (Sumter is near historic Camden, S.C.) For information, write Sumter Chamber of Commerce, P.O. Drawer 1229, Sumter, SC 29150, or the Sumter Parks and Recreation Department.

Meiji Shrine, Tokyo. (Japan Travel Bureau)

Tennessee

Memphis

Japanese Garden in Memphis Botanic Garden

The Japanese garden is a beautiful, restful spot in this 88-acre Memphis Botanic Garden. It was designed by Dr. Takuma P. Tono of Tokyo.

The garden is planned to surround Lake Biwa, named for the body of water in the famous Lake Biwa National Park of Japan. The Japanese are very fond of a musical instrument called the "biwa," shaped like the loquat or biwa fruit. This is similar to a mandolin in shape—as is the lake in Japan, and now the one in Tennessee!

The bridge in Memphis Botanic Garden's Japanese garden. (Ken Ross)

There is a gracefully curved red bridge crossing the lake at one point, and a peaceful "moon-gazing pavilion." Carefully placed rocks and lanterns add interest along the shore. This Japanese garden was created by the Memphis Park Commission with the cooperation of the Bamboo Chapter of Ikebana International.

Memphis Botanic Garden has other points of interest such as some 4000 roses in one garden, and gardens with many varieties of irises, dahlias and wildflowers. In the splendid Michie Magnolia Garden one may see many of the varieties which originated in China and Japan, blooming in March and April. The Conservatory, Orchid House and Camellia House are a joy in the more wintry months.

OPEN: Daily, 8 a.m. to sundown. The Goldsmith Civic Garden Center is open Mon. through Fri., 9 a.m. to 5 p.m., and Sun. 2 to 5 p.m.

ADMISSION: Free.

ADDRESS: Memphis Botanic Garden, 750 Cherry Rd., Memphis, TN 38117. Telephone: 901-685-1566.

DIRECTIONS: The garden is located about 9 miles from downtown Memphis.

Nashville

Japanese Tea Garden at the Tennessee Botanical Gardens

A small Japanese tea garden, modeled after those of Japan in the sixteenth and seventeenth centuries, is a new attractive feature at the entrance to Botanic Hall here. It was designed by Coleman (Mrs. James B.) Helme, who also executed it herself with the enthusiastic aid of her son and several interested friends. Conceived as a showcase for a collection of dwarf junipers and other slow-growing evergreens, it has a wonderful variety of heights and textures, as can be seen by studying the plan in our illustration. Although there are various shades of green in the plants chosen, as well as some color from a pink dogwood, azaleas, rhododendrons and a weeping cherry, the arrangement was deliberately kept in

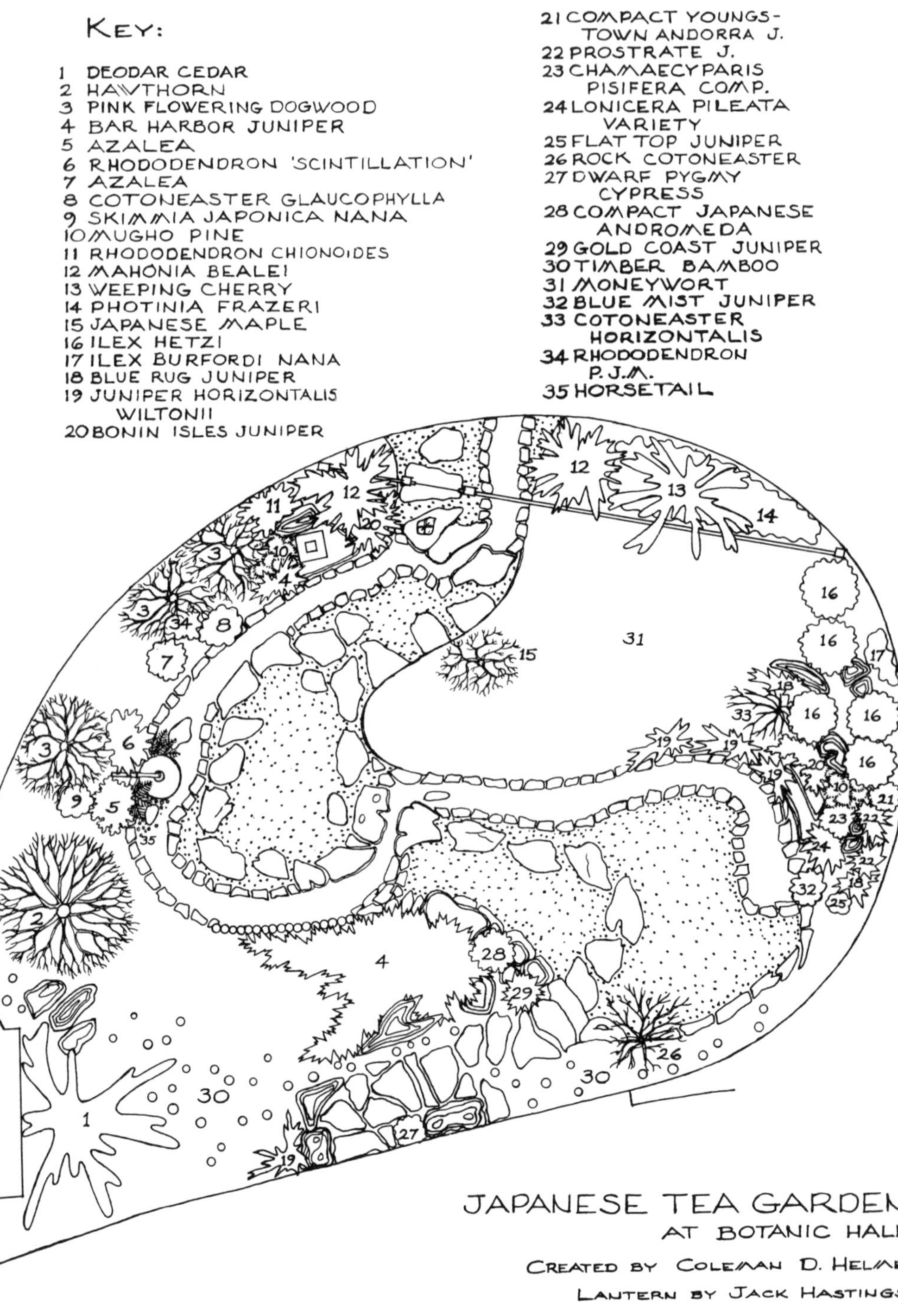

KEY:

1 DEODAR CEDAR
2 HAWTHORN
3 PINK FLOWERING DOGWOOD
4 BAR HARBOR JUNIPER
5 AZALEA
6 RHODODENDRON 'SCINTILLATION'
7 AZALEA
8 COTONEASTER GLAUCOPHYLLA
9 SKIMMIA JAPONICA NANA
10 MUGHO PINE
11 RHODODENDRON CHIONOIDES
12 MAHONIA BEALEI
13 WEEPING CHERRY
14 PHOTINIA FRAZERI
15 JAPANESE MAPLE
16 ILEX HETZI
17 ILEX BURFORDI NANA
18 BLUE RUG JUNIPER
19 JUNIPER HORIZONTALIS WILTONII
20 BONIN ISLES JUNIPER
21 COMPACT YOUNGSTOWN ANDORRA J.
22 PROSTRATE J.
23 CHAMAECYPARIS PISIFERA COMP.
24 LONICERA PILEATA VARIETY
25 FLAT TOP JUNIPER
26 ROCK COTONEASTER
27 DWARF PYGMY CYPRESS
28 COMPACT JAPANESE ANDROMEDA
29 GOLD COAST JUNIPER
30 TIMBER BAMBOO
31 MONEYWORT
32 BLUE MIST JUNIPER
33 COTONEASTER HORIZONTALIS
34 RHODODENDRON P.J.M.
35 HORSETAIL

JAPANESE TEA GARDEN
AT BOTANIC HALL
CREATED BY COLEMAN D. HELME
LANTERN BY JACK HASTINGS

subdued shades, with materials which will age well into that appearance of timelessness which the Japanese value so highly.

From a miniature dry "waterfall" of rocks, a pebbled stream bed winds through a lower area between high embankments. The stepping stone path ends at a rustic thatch-roofed gate in a bamboo fence. Beside this stands a traditional stone lantern created by Jack Hastings. Truly a little gem among Japanese gardens!

A second Japanese garden, eventually covering about four acres, and to be called the Japanese Stroll Garden is just being started here. It was inspired by the vision and generosity of Mrs. George Weesner, former president of Ikebana International Chapter 5 (who is now president of the Tennessee Federation of Garden Clubs). She made a large donation toward creation of this new garden, on condition that an equal amount be raised for it by the Ikebana chapter. Mr. Kingsley K. Wu of Perdue University is the design consultant for this project.

The bamboo gate and fence serve as background to the new Japanese tea garden at Botanic Hall. (Randall E. Lantz)

The Japanese stroll garden will include a small dry Zen meditation area with a stone "waterfall," beach and dock. The remainder of the garden will have paths up and down the slopes, a pond, and several structures still to be decided upon. It will have two main entrance gates.

OPEN: Tennessee Botanical Gardens are open Tues. through Sat., 10 a.m. to 5 p.m.; Sun., 1 to 5 p.m. Closed on Thanksgiving, Christmas and New Year's Day.

ADMISSION: Adults 50¢; children 25¢.

ADDRESS: Tennessee Botanical Gardens and Fine Arts Center, Cheekwood, Cheek Rd., Nashville, TN 37205. Telephone: 615-356-3306.

DIRECTIONS: The gardens are 7 miles west of Nashville on Cheek Rd., off Rte. 100.

Texas

Austin

Taniguchi Oriental Garden

"It has been my wish that through the construction of this garden I might provide a symbol of universal peace . . . My desire for the peace of mankind . . . endowed this man of old age the physical health and stamina to pile stone upon stone without a day's absence for the last eighteen months . . . to complete this long-dreamed gift for the city of Austin—this Oriental Garden." So wrote Mr. Isamu Taniguchi in an essay called "The Spirit of the Garden" (translated from Japanese by Mrs. Y. S. Jolly). It was his vision and his own dedicated hard labor which created this beautiful spot in Austin's Zilker Park. He had wanted to name the garden "Friendship Hands Across the Sea," but it is most appropriate that it now bears the name of its creator.

Mr. Taniguchi was born in Japan in 1887, came to the United States at the age of seventeen, and returned to his homeland only once to claim the bride his family had selected for him. After farming in California for many years, he chose to retire in 1967 in Austin where his son had attended the University of Texas. There he began his unpaid labor of love for his adopted city.

He transformed three acres of rugged cliffs into a beautiful, tranquil garden which gives pleasure to some 100,000 visitors each year. The central feature is a lotus pond with an island and a "rainbow bridge." Nearby a fifteen-foot-high waterfall provides dramatic sight and sound, flowing into a second pool. Many stone lanterns—gifts from various garden clubs—decorate the paths. Hundreds of cherry trees along the lake make a breathtaking spectacle in the spring with their confetti of pink blossoms.

At the entrance to the park stands the fine building of the Austin Area Garden Center. This, too, is an example of dedication by many hundreds of garden lovers. Thirty-one garden clubs (members of the National Council of State Garden Clubs) raised over $78,000 to build and furnish the center. Some 40,000 people a year use its many facilities and attend meetings there. For each visitor, the Taniguchi Oriental Garden is a special joy.

OPEN: Daily, 10 a.m. to 4:45 p.m.

ADMISSION: Free.

ADDRESS: Austin Area Garden Center, Inc., 2220 Barton Springs Rd., Austin, TX 78746. Telephone: 512-477-8672.

MAINTAINED BY: Austin Parks and Recreation Board.

Dallas

Japanese Garden at Royal Tokyo Restaurant

An authentic Japanese garden is not often built in one week, even when it is as small as this one is. However, that is what happened here in the fall of 1973, due to the expertise and excellent preparatory work of its designer, Nobuya Kimya Hira. Born and educated in Japan, he had exceptionally thorough training in the art of Japanese garden design, holding degrees both in architecture and landscape architecture from Tokyo Horticultural University. After his graduation he spent another one and a half years studying these subjects at the University of Washington in Seattle. In Japan his eminent instructor was Professor Takuma Tono, who designed the outstanding Japanese garden in Portland, Oregon. Professor Tono insisted that his students spend hours in the field observing how nature's waterfalls were constructed, how pine trees became twisted into artistic shapes by the winds, and the arrangement of rocks where they had fallen, untouched by human hands.

Kimya Hira, the son of two doctors, has kept himself in excellent physical condition, holding the black belt rank in both karate and judo. So driving to Dallas from California in a truck filled with just the right trees, shrubs and plants, and then heaving boulders many times heavier than himself for a week with his two assistants, did not prove too difficult for him. He is amused when he remembers that it was his garden-loving karate teacher who led him into the work of a landscape architect.

This small Japanese garden at the Royal Tokyo Restaurant has a fine waterfall splashing over lichen-covered rocks into a pond filled with *koi* (carp). The bridge leads into the restaurant. Carefully placed evergreens, ground covers and stone lanterns complete the authentic design—a refreshing sight on a hot Texas day.

ADDRESS: Royal Tokyo Restaurant, 7525 Greenville St., Dallas, TX 75200. Telephone: 214-368-3304.

Dallas

Japanese Garden in Kidd Springs Park

A Japanese garden beside the lake was added to Kidd Springs Park in 1969 by the Dallas Park and Recreation Department. Designed by Maylon Perry, member of a local landscaping firm, it features an imposing red *torii* standing in the water—a scene familiar to all tourists to Japan. This and many other ancient Japanese art objects were the gifts of Dr. and Mrs. Jack F. Edwards of Oak Cliff. These gifts include the following: a Buddhist temple bell from the Hosenji Temple, hanging in a replica of an authentic bell tower; a red bridge, copied from the famous one in Nikko, reserved exclusively there for the use of priests; a roofed entrance gate; tons of stone lanterns originally sent by the Japanese government for exhibit at the Century of Progress Exposition in Chicago in 1933; several stone Buddhas at least 200 years old; and twelve painted wooden lanterns. The garden is being constantly improved with the assistance of the Japanese-American community.

OPEN: Daily.

ADMISSION: Free.

ADDRESS: 711 W. Canty St., Dallas, TX 75200.

MAINTAINED BY: Dallas Park and Recreation Department, City Hall. Telephone: 214-748-9711, Ext. 247.

Fort Worth

Fort Worth Japanese Garden

The Japanese garden at Fort Worth, opened to the public in 1973, is a beautiful one with some unusual points of interest. It was designed by Mr. Kingsley Wu who was educated in Tokyo, but is now at the University of Perdue (formerly Texas Women's University) in its Department of Environmental Design. The topography of the 7½ acres was retained in as natural a state as possible, and many of the original trees were incorporated into the plan so that it already has a settled look which is very pleasing. New trees were contributed by the City of Arlington Park Department, and by the Muskogee, Oklahoma Park Department. The Men's Garden Club of Ft. Worth donated and planted fifteen oaks.

The winding paths, mainly of patterned stone, lead in and out through woodsy areas, past three separate ponds where Japanese painted mandarin ducks nest in a special home made of cork oak bark, on a post above the water. One of the pools contains many

Above, one of the teahouses; below, the pool with peckerel weed and yellow flag iris. (Mike C. Williams)

colorful *koi* (carp). Several small cascades and waterfalls fill the air with their magic. An unusual feature is a group of five teahouses, one of them (a memorial gift) including authentic furnishings. Eventually it is hoped that tea and cookies may be served there.

The flat stone-and-gravel meditation garden is similar to the famous one at Ryoan-ji Temple in Kyoto. It is said to be most beautiful when a fine mist is falling, or after a rain. In another part of the garden there is a "moon deck" where children play in the daytime, and adults set up instruments to study the universe at night. This is certainly a practical American version of the Japanese moon-viewing platforms which were designed only for absorbing the moon's beauty!

One striking ornamental feature is a pagoda designed by the Komatsu Architectural Firm, and built by park employees. It is thirty-three feet high, of iron inside, with copper roof. It can be seen from many parts of the garden. The pagoda and the plantings around it were given as memorials, as were many stone lanterns throughout the grounds, including two from local chapter 38 of Ikebana International. Many garden clubs and other community organizations have contributed to the beauty of this place. Even the ornamental stones—some 4 million pounds—were a gift, from the Nivens and Hollaway families of Alvord, Texas. (They were hauled fifty-six miles from Alvord to their present site.) Slate-covered benches at many points invite visitors to pause, relax, and absorb the interesting views.

OPEN: Tues. to Fri., 10 a.m. to 4 p.m.; Sat., 10 a.m. to 5 p.m.; Sun., 1 to 5 p.m. Closed on Mon.

ADMISSION: $1.00 per person, 12 and over; children under 12, free when accompanied by an adult. Picnic area in adjacent Trinity Park.

ADDRESS: 3220 Botanic Garden Dr., Ft. Worth, TX 76107.

CONTACT FOR INFORMATION: Ft. Worth Botanic Garden Center. Telephone: 817-737-3330.

MAINTAINED BY: City of Fort Worth.

DIRECTIONS: Take East-West Freeway westbound to University Dr. exit, then go north to Botanic Garden Dr.

Utah

Salt Lake City

International Peace Gardens

The International Peace Gardens, located in Jordan Park, are the result of a project initiated in 1939 by the Salt Lake Council of Women. Inspired by their citizenship chairwoman, Mrs. Otto A. Wiesley, they invited citizens of foreign ancestry to join in creating gardens typical of their countries of origin. They wanted to show that people of all nations could cooperate to create peace. Unfortunately all work had to be curtailed during World War II, but was resumed with enthusiasm in 1947. Each national group planned, financed and built its own garden, then turned it over to the city parks department for maintenance.

Today there are eighteen nations represented, including three of Oriental origin. India has no garden, but the government of India sent a very fine bronze statue of the "Preaching Buddha" as its contribution.

The Chinese garden, completed in 1953, is located near the entrance. It was designed by Alfred K. Mong, a young graduate of the engineering school of State University in Salt Lake City, and his assistants. Its main point of interest is a handsome red triple-roofed pagoda and a curved bridge over a winding pool. A willow tree and a magnolia (symbol of peace to the Chinese) are prominent in the plantings. Chinese poems are inscribed on the entrance gate.

The Japanese garden, dedicated in the summer of 1950, was the first one to be completed here. It was financed with individual contributions from all the intermountain states, and fund raising by the local Japanese community. Two professional gardeners were sent by the Japanese consular office in San Francisco to design it. Through the aid of General Douglas MacArthur, four ancient stone lanterns from the emperor's Palace Gardens were shipped from Japan. A small bronze statue of the Goddess Kuan Yin also came from Tokyo, where it had survived two bombings.

A section of the Japanese garden. (Mark Meyer)

The teahouse and *torii* gate were donated by the consulate's office after being exhibited at the Seattle World's Fair.

There is a pretty red bridge over a pool, surrounded by evergreen shrubs which are kept clipped in the traditional tiered "cloud pruning" style. All along the River Jordan there are Japanese cherries abloom in the spring, the gift of Japanese Boy Scouts. One tree was planted and dedicated in 1974 by the mayor of Matsumoto, which has a Sister City relationship with Salt Lake City.

The other countries represented in these beautiful International Peace Gardens with typical flowers and structures are America, Britain, Canada, Denmark, Finland, Germany, Greece, Holland, Italy, Lebanon, Mexico, Norway, Sweden, Switzerland and Wales. Other nations are invited to participate at any time by demonstrating their garden heritage. This is a wonderful example of

Bridge and pagoda in the Chinese garden. (Mark Meyer)

understanding and cooperation among the many nationalities which make up the citizenry of our United States.

OPEN: Daily, May through Sept.

ADMISSION: Free.

ADDRESS: The Gardens are at 10th South St. and 8th West St. in Jordan Park. Salt Lake City Parks Department: City and County Building, Salt Lake City, UT 84109. Telephone: 801-328-7838.

Virginia

Norfolk

Japanese Garden in Norfolk Botanical Gardens

The Japanese garden is a small but interesting 1/2 acre section in the Norfolk Botanical Gardens (which cover 175 acres). Designed by the staff from pictures and plans of an obscure garden in Japan, it was opened to the public in 1962. A gravel bottomed "dry stream" has a bright red bridge over it, and there is a square stone *mizubachi* water basin. A large *yukimi* lantern was donated by Norfolk's Japanese Sister City Moji and another ornament is a smaller "firefly" lantern. Camellias, crabapples, wisteria and cherry trees show their colors in the spring, while red Japanese maples furnish accents in the fall. The main paths are of asphalt instead of the usual stepping stones, to make it easier for visitors in wheelchairs or with strollers to enjoy the garden.

The Norfolk Botanical Gardens are famous for their annual International Azalea Festival, and their glorious plantings of camellias and rhododendrons.

OPEN: 8:30 a.m. to sundown, daily.

ADMISSION: 15¢ per person. Narrated tours on small open trains are available, the 30-minute ride costing 75¢, the one-hour ride $1.50. There are also five canal boats for 21 passengers each, for 30-minute rides at $1.00 per person.

ADDRESS: Norfolk Botanical Gardens, Airport Rd., Norfolk, VA 23518. Telephone: 703-853-6972.

MAINTAINED BY: The City of Norfolk.

DIRECTIONS: Follow Airport signs; the gardens are located just off Rte. 170.

Red bridge over the dry stream bed in the Japanese garden at Norfolk Botanical Gardens. (G.W. Baker)

Richmond

The Japanese Garden at Maymont

When Major James Henry Dooley traveled about the world with his wife in the early 1900s, they became enchanted with the gardens they saw in two very different countries—Italy and Japan. Upon settling in Richmond on their 105-acre estate, where they built a great stone Victorian mansion with many outbuildings, they had two special gardens laid out there: a large one in Italian style, which has already been restored to its original beauty; and a Japanese garden (350 by 600 feet), for which they imported a landscape architect and workmen from Japan.

This lovely Japanese-style garden is now being restored at great cost by the Maymont Foundation for the city of Richmond, which owns the property willed to it by Major Dooley. It lies just below the Italian garden on a slope between the James River and the Kanawaha Canal. Its main feature at present is a splendid

90-foot waterfall with cascades pouring into a reflecting pool. There is a large stone grotto, and groves of bamboo among other plants which were originally brought from Japan. A teahouse is being planned to replace one which vanished over the years.

Major Dooley was a member of the Virginia legislature and a financier interested chiefly in railroads. This beautiful estate which he caused to be created on a former cow pasture is now, due to his generosity, a fascinating point of interest for anyone visiting historic Richmond.

OPEN: Daily, from 10 a.m. to sundown.

ADMISSION: Free.

ADDRESS: Maymont, 1700 Hampton St., Richmond, VA 23220. Telephone: 804-358-7166.

Washington

Bellevue

Yao Park, Sister City Oriental Garden

This Oriental garden was inspired by the decision in 1970 to form a Sister City relationship between Bellevue and the city of Yao in Japan, which had almost the same population and similar trends in its growth. Bellevue wanted to create a garden with Oriental flavor as a visual and lasting monument to international friendship. Two acres were set aside for this in the eighty-acre community park which was then under construction. Landscape architect Siegfried A. Semrau, director of Parks and Recreation for the city, was the designer.

A small stream found on one boundary was diverted, deepened, and fed into a number of new ponds as it wound through the garden. Several bridges were constructed, two of weathered cedar and one painted dark red. In one pond there is a small observation platform jutting out over the water among plantings of fishpole bamboo, wild yellow iris and cattails. Beyond, Western hemlocks and lodge pole pines are mirrored in the quiet waters.

The entrance courtyard has a small open cedar shelter and a fine Japanese stone lantern, presented by officials from the city of Yao to Bellevue's Mayor Gates at the opening ceremonies in 1972. The stepping stone paths throughout the garden are surrounded by lingonberry ground cover. Occasional color is seen in the spring when azaleas, crabapples and rhododendrons are in bloom. Glorious fall color is the result of careful plantings of sweetgums, vine maples and red cutleaf maples.

Left, the cedar shelter; right, the Japanese lantern. (Frank M. Anderson)

This tranquil garden with its native northwestern trees and shrubs has been given a true Oriental atmosphere for those who are seeking the refreshing beauty of nature. It is the outcome of splendid cooperation by many youth groups and local residents who donated both plants and labor to assist the Department of Parks and Recreation. The result is that there is no vandalism, and young and old alike appreciate this new and lovely place.

OPEN: Daily, 7 a.m. to 10 p.m.

ADMISSION: Free.

ADDRESS: 13204 S.E. 8th St., Bellevue, WA 98009. For information, write Bellevue Department of Parks & Recreation, P.O. Box 1768, Bellevue, WA 98009. Telephone: 206-455-6881.

Seattle

Japanese Garden of the University of Washington

Hills and a lake, framed in lavender wisteria—that is how visitors remember this lovely garden (see dust jacket). The Japanese garden of the University of Washington Arboretum, completed in 1960, was designed by Mr. Juki Iida of Tokyo, an outstanding landscape architect of over 1000 gardens. He supervised every step of the construction together with his assistant, Mr. T. Kitamura. The garden covers about 3½ acres and is unusual in many ways. The higher "mountain" area is covered with forest, a backdrop for an eleven-story stone pagoda. From here two streams emerge to form a waterfall and run into a lake. The teahouse, a gift from the city of Tokyo which represented a "mountain villa" on high ground, was destroyed by fire and has not yet been replaced. The little garden around it contained the traditional waiting booth, stone purification basin and lantern.

Cliffs follow along the lake shore, where there is a pebble beach, a moon-viewing platform, and the lovely wisteria arbor. Mr. Iida conceived of this area as a small "fishing village." Eventually the Arboretum hopes to build a clubhouse here. Rock islands in the lake are connected by bridges. A lantern on one of these islands is to "illuminate snow falling during the night." On the central isle the designer placed a gate similar to one at the famous Shugaku-in Temple in Kyoto. Iris and water lilies decorate the quiet pond. An *azumaya* or resting place on the higher slope allows visitors to enjoy another fine view, including a grove of flowering plums and cherries at one side.

Ten beautiful stone lanterns of various types decorate the paths. The very ornamental *Todo-gata* was the gift of Seattle's Sister City Kobe in Japan. It symbolizes earth, water, fire, wind and sky. The inscription on its pedestal reads: "May the light shine everlastingly on the friendship between Kobe and Seattle." A very unusual lantern is the *Okazaki-gata* or turtle lantern (named for the city of Okazaki). This has a carved turtle for a base. Here, too, one may see an example of the so-called "Christian lantern" created by Turuta Oribe (1542-1615) who was a great philosopher, master of tea ceremony, and landscape designer. The lantern has a sculptured figure representing the Virgin Mary.

It is difficult to realize that the two "mountains" here are entirely man-made, and that the hundreds of rocks—many weighing as much as eight tons—were all brought in from the outside. The entire scene looks completely natural. It is a beautiful combination of serene Japanese garden and northwestern American forest.

OPEN: Daily, 10 a.m. to dusk, Apr. to mid-Nov. In winter, only on weekends.

ADMISSION: Free.

ADDRESS: University of Washington Arboretum, Seattle, WA 98105. Telephone: 206-543-8800.

MAINTAINED BY: The College of Forest Resources, with donations from individuals.

DIRECTIONS: The Arboretum is about a 20-minute walk from the university campus. Entrance from Lake Washington Blvd.

*Top, the wisteria arbor and Omokaga-gata lantern; bottom, a view of the lake.
(George Taloumis)*

Spokane

Oriental Garden

This Oriental garden was designed by the late Sugiero Kubota, head of the family's landscaping firm, in 1929. There are twenty acres in all, the Oriental feature comprising about four acres. It is a lovely garden including waterfalls and streams, imported Japanese lanterns, and a simple *azumaya* (resting shelter). The Kubota brothers, who now head the organization, have been most generous in allowing garden clubs, school classes and individuals to visit the garden, and in giving them an interesting guided tour.

OPEN (by appointment only): Telephone 206-725-4400, or 206-722-6868.

ADDRESS: 9817 55th Ave. South, Seattle, WA 98118.

Spokane

Manito Japanese Garden

The story of the creation of this garden is a heartwarming one, touching, sad, but also supremely inspiring. It could well serve as an example to all other communities and organizations that might become discouraged in trying to promote a new garden.

It goes back to 1962, when Spokane formed a Sister City link with the Japanese city of Nishinomiya. The site of 1½ acres was chosen by that city's mayor, Tatsuo Tatsuuma. The garden had been a dream of many years of Mrs. Polly Mitchell Judd, an enthusiastic gardener who was active in garden clubs throughout the area. She and her husband, a professional surveyor, made a detail map of the land in 1969.

Mr. Nagao Sakurai, well-known landscape architect, was engaged that year to design the garden. He was a graduate and later a professor of Tokyo University for many years, and had been supervisor of the Imperial Palace Gardens for another fifteen years. Later he was to plan Japanese gardens from coast to coast in America. Some are included in this book: the California gardens at

---

The waterfall in Manito Japanese Garden. (Kathy Mathison)

Upper left, the island with its Bonza tree, two bronze cranes, and a live turtle; upper right, bronze temple lantern, cast in Japan in 1914; below, an azumaya. (Photos by Kathy Mathison)

Lodi, Los Angeles (UCLA), San Francisco's Classical Garden in Golden Gate Park, San Mateo, and the garden in Hilo, Hawaii. He also had designed a garden for the first New York World's Fair—in fact, a total of 160 gardens.

When work on Spokane's garden began in 1967, Mr. Sakurai was already seventy years old. He spoke no English, but communicated with the workmen of the park department through sketches and gestures. He planned the whole garden in his mind instead of making a detail drawing of it in its entirety. He knew exactly where he wanted each stone to go, what trees should be removed, how the new pond should be shaped. Mr. Arnold Gehrke of the park department, who worked on the project throughout its construction, remembers with a smile that his workmen had to change the position of a rock twenty-three times before Mr. Sakurai, a perfectionist, was satisfied. Every stone had to be old and moss-covered. Through occasional interpreters he communicated his enthusiasm for this site where he hoped to create his "dream garden," the finest of them all.

Then, in 1970, three years after he had been engaged to supervise the garden, he was felled by a stroke which paralyzed one whole side. He was transferred to a nursing home—even underwent some surgery—but he would not give up. Though he could not be out of bed for more than two or three hours a day, he was taken to the site by his dedicated friend, Polly Mitchell Judd, and sat there in a wheelchair making precise drawings so that the work could go on. He sketched the lanterns to be made by a local artisan; where the teahouse would go; what plants should be placed or removed. Mrs. Judd made a detailed map, and took over 1000 Polaroid pictures to show him in the nursing home, so that he could see each step of the operations and make suggestions. His son, Kenichi Sakurai, came from San Francisco and directed the design of the fence as his father wanted it.

His relatives in Japan apparently were too concerned about him to let him stay in America. He was suddenly sent home by air—only to catch pneumonia and die there six weeks later. It is tragic to think that this gentle old genius could never see his work completed in Spokane. The garden is still not finished. Yet from its very beginning, hundreds of people have had a share in its increasing beauty. There have been donations from the Associated

Garden Clubs of Spokane and many other clubs; the city's Japanese community; the Sister City Committee; the women of Rotary; school children—the list is almost endless. The Sister City of Nishinomiya sent $1000 raised from a bazaar, and the brass finials for the ceremonial bridge posts which were shipped free by Japan Airlines. Contractors and army engineers have donated labor. After Mr. Sakurai's death, landscape architects from Kobe, Japan, went on with the construction. Dignitaries from the two Sister Cities formally dedicated the garden in May 1974.

This is a stroll garden of great beauty and serenity. The splashing of the waterfall can be heard throughout, due to a special sound chamber built into the rocks. The various bridges have different types of ornamental railings. An *azumaya* (resting shelter) is placed where visitors may relax and absorb the peaceful sights and sounds. A beautiful *Kasuga* lantern over 100 years old was the gift of industrialist Matashiro Shibakawa of Nishinomiya. The two bronze temple lanterns had been cast in 1914, and were used in Japan to designate the first place for prayer.

Landscape architect Nagao Sakurai, studying placement of rocks and a lantern. (Polly Mitchell Judd)

Every turn of the paths, every rock shape, each place of beauty should remind the visitor to this Manito Japanese Garden of the artistic vision and persistence of Nagao Sakurai, and the dedication and selfless devotion of his friend, Polly Mitchell Judd, without whom there would have been no garden. One can only hope that as the work goes on to complete Sakurai's dream, it will be done as he had wished it—a memorial to a great landscape designer.

OPEN: Daily, 8 a.m. to dusk.

ADMISSION: Free.

ADDRESS OF GARDEN: Bernard St. and 21st St., Spokane. Address of Spokane Park and Recreation Department: Room 504, City Hall, Spokane, WA 99201. Telephone: 509-456-2620.

MAINTAINED BY: Spokane City Park Department and the Manito Japanese Garden Association.

Tacoma

Japanese Garden in Point Defiance Park

Residents of Tacoma have long been grateful to the citizens of 1888 who set aside 640 acres for this Point Defiance Park, formerly a military reservation. More than a million visitors come each year to enjoy its recreational facilities. Since 1965, an added attraction has been the small Japanese garden (about 1½ acres) planned by Howard S. Harmon, director of horticulture of the Metropolitan Park Department.

Here cascading waterfalls pour into a meandering stream which fills two ponds, spanned by a natural wood bridge. Japanese red pine, Hinoki cypress and *Pieris japonica* are among the evergreens planted as background, while rhododendrons and azaleas are bright in the spring and scarlet Japanese maples are aflame in the fall. A "dry river" with large boulders spurs the imagination in the traditional Japanese way, as do the "cloud-pruned" evergreens. Three splendid specimens of *Sequoia gigantea*, over fifty years old, add a feeling of age and permanence.

Japanese garden in Point Defiance Park. (Metropolitan Park District of Tacoma)

The upper part of the garden provides a magnificent view of Puget Sound, almost as far as Seattle. At the east boundary a large two-story pagoda building houses practical facilities, as well as the headquarters of the Capitol District of Garden Clubs. All these clubs contributed generously to the planting of this peaceful garden spot.

OPEN: Daily till dark.

ADMISSION: Free.

ADDRESS: Entrance to Point Defiance Park is at the end of Pearl Street; the Japanese Garden is in the central area.

MAINTAINED BY: Metropolitan Park District, 236 County-City Bldg., Tacoma, WA 98409. Telephone: 206-759-8456.

Annotated Bibliography

I. ORIENTAL INFLUENCES ON GARDENS IN EUROPE AND AMERICA

A. *Oriental Plant Introductions:*

Anderson, A. W. *How We Got Our Flowers.* New York: Dover, 1966. Amusing stories about English plant collectors in the Orient, with a special chapter on "Golden Flowers from China"—the chrysanthemum.

Cox, E. H. M. *Plant Hunting in China..* London: Oldbourne, 1945. Very fascinating accounts of the best-known plant hunters of Britain, Europe and America.

Farrington, Edward I. *Ernest H. Wilson, Plant Hunter.* Boston: Stratford, 1931. The fascinating story of the greatest of the plant hunters, his adventures while obtaining hundreds of plant introductions from China, Japan, etc.

The Shell Garden Book. London: Phoenix House, 1964. Interesting short biographies of some famous English plant explorers.

Sirén, Osvald. *China and the Gardens of Europe of the Eighteenth Century.* New York: Ronald Press, 1950. Includes some data on flowers originating in China.

B.   *Oriental Influences on Gardens*

Erdberg, Eleanor von. *Chinese Influence on European Garden Structures.* Boston: Harvard University Press, 1936. Delightful drawings of Chinese pagodas, pavilions, etc., from European gardens. The appendix describes gardens with Chinese influence in ten countries, including Russia, and tells which of these could still be seen in 1936.

Lancaster, Craig. *The Japanese Influence in America.* New York: Rawls, 1963. Chapter XVII is on "Japanese Gardens and Landscaping in America," giving the history of the earliest ones in expositions and on private estates. Many photographs.

McFadden, Dorothy Loa. *Gardens of Europe, A Pictorial Tour.* South Brunswick and New York: Barnes, 1970. There are 169 photographs, some in color, including six of Japanese gardens in Europe.

McFadden, Dorothy Loa. *Touring the Gardens of Europe.* New York: McKay, 1965. A traveler's guide to over 800 gardens in eighteen countries, including some of Japanese inspiration.

The Shell Garden Book. London: Phoenix House, 1964. Includes a section on Chinese garden structures in Great Britain.

II. TRADITIONAL GARDENS IN CHINA, INDIA, IRAN AND JAPAN

Ayscough, Florence. *A Chinese Mirror.* New York: Houghton Mifflin, 1925. A book on Chinese customs, philosophy, etc., including a delightful chapter on "The Chinese Idea of a Garden." Illustrated with excellent pen-and-ink drawings by Lucille Douglass.

Berrall, Julia S. *The Garden, An Illustrated History.* New York: Viking, 1966. Probably the most complete and certainly the most beautifully illustrated history of gardens. Includes chapters on China, Iran and Japan.

Burland, Cottie A. *The Travels of Marco Polo.* New York: McGraw-Hill, 1970. Excerpts from Marco Polo's accounts of his visit to China, illustrated by superb color photographs by Werner Forman, of the places as they look today. See plates 36, 43, 45, 54, 55 and 62 for gardens still to be seen.

Charageat, Marguerite. *L'Art des Jardins.* Paris: Presses Universitaires de France, 1962. Very well-researched chapters (all in French) on gardens of China, Iran and Japan. Many fine photographs.

Chimay, Jacqueline. *Les Jardins a Travers le Monde.* Paris: Hachette, 1962. Excellent histories (in French) of gardens in China, India, Iran and Japan. Many fine photographs.

Danby, Hope. *The Garden of Perfect Brightness.* Chicago: Regnery, 1950. A dramatically written history of three Chinese Emperors (1662-1860) with the famous palace gardens of Yüan Ming Yüan as the center of interest.

Engel, David H. *Japanese Gardens for Today.* Tokyo and Rutland, Vt.: Tuttle, 1959. Suggestions by an expert landscape designer on how to make a Japanese garden in the West, suited to today's needs. Illustrated with superb photographs of private and public gardens in Japan. List of suitable plants.

Froncek, Thomas (Managing Editor). *The Horizon Book of the Arts of China.* New York: American Heritage Press, 1969. See a short chapter on "The Garden Retreat"; another on "The Palace of the Emperor." Very beautiful photographs.

Gothein, Marie Luise. *A History of Garden Art,* translated from the German by Mrs. Archer-Hind. London: J. M. Dent & Sons, 1928. 2 Vols. A very comprehensive history with many illustrations.

Graham, Dorothy. *Chinese Gardens.* New York: Dodd Mead, 1938. The author describes many individual gardens she saw in China before 1938, in Hangchow, Soochow, Shanghai, Peking, Yangchow. Many photographs.

Horizon Magazine. New York: American Heritage Press, issue of May, 1959. Pictures of India, Iran, Japan.

Howard, Edwin L. *Chinese Garden Architecture.* New York: Macmillan, 1931. Very fine photographs.

Hyams, Edward. *A History of Gardens and Gardening.* New York: Praeger, 1971. Scholarly research on history, and excellent horticultural data, including China, Iran and Japan. Many illustrations.

Inn, Henry, and other authors. *Chinese Houses and Gardens.* New York: Hastings, 1940. Excellent authentic material by authorities, plus beautiful photographs by Henry Inn.

Ishimoto, Tatsuo. *The Art of the Japanese Garden.* New York: Crown, 1958. Suggestions and plans for making a

Japanese garden, with over 200 excellent photographs of details in gardens of Japan.

Japan, the Official Guide. Tokyo: Tourist Industry Bureau, 1961. An excellent, very detailed guide; Chapter XIX is on "Landscape and Other Gardening."

Kincaid, Mrs. Paul. *Japanese Garden and Floral Art.* New York: Hearthside Press, 1966. An extremely clear, well-organized book giving all the essential information about Japanese garden art, symbolism, decorative features, etc.; with a special section on designing such gardens for America, and another with tips for travelers to Japan.

Kuck, Loraine E. *The Art of the Japanese Garden.* New York: John Day, 1940. Still the most detailed and authoritative book on the subject, with a poetically written history through the ages. Includes two chapters on the gardens of old China. Many good photographs.

Powell, Florence Lee. *In the Chinese Garden.* New York: John Day, 1943. A step-by-step tour through the Liu Yuan and Shih Tzu Lin gardens in Soochow. Photographs, plans, details and explanations of symbolism.

Randhawa, M. S. *Beautiful Trees and Gardens.* Calcutta: Sree Saraswaty Press, 1961. A blending of poetry and information, with emphasis on the myths, legends and poems about the trees of India; also chapters on the Hindu-Buddhist garden, Persian and Moghul gardens, tree festivals in India, gardens of Japan, and the origin of plants.

Randhawa, M. S. *The Cult of Trees and Tree Worship in Buddhist-Hindu Sculpture.* New Delhi: All India Fine Arts & Crafts Society, 1964. A fascinating photographic book of these sculptures dating up to the thirteenth century, with a final chapter on "Tree Worship in Present-Day India."

Sirén, Osvald. *Gardens of China.* New York: Ronald Press, 1949. Informal reminiscences of the author's travels in

Peking and Soochow in 1922, 1929 and 1935, with his own photographs. Includes a chapter on the older gardens of Japan which showed the Chinese influence. The drawings of balustrades, window lattices, ornamental doorways, etc., should be most useful to anyone interested in creating a Chinese garden.

Steele, Fletcher. *Gardens and People.* New York: Houghton Mifflin, 1964. Includes a delightful chapter on gardens of China.

Takakuwa, Gisei. *Invitation to Japanese Gardens.* Tokyo and Rutland, Vt.: Tuttle, 1970. A guide to the best gardens to be seen in Japan, arranged geographically, with superb photographs by Kiichi Asano. Informative captions explain the design and historic period of each garden. Together with the garden map of Japan and another just of Kyoto, this is a gold mine for garden-oriented travelers as well as students of Japanese garden design.

Tatsui, Matsunosuke. *Japanese Gardens.* Tokyo: Japan Travel Bureau, 1962. A small book full of information, history and descriptions of gardens to be seen today in Japan, with fine photographs.

Wheeler, Mortimer E. *Splendors of the East.* London: Spring Books, 1965. Superbly illustrated in color, includes four chapters on China.

Whittle, Tyler. *Some Ancient Gentlemen.* New York: Taplinger, 1966. Some amusing notes on gardens of China.

Wilber, Donald N. *Persian Gardens and Garden Pavilions.* Tokyo and Rutland, Vt.: Tuttle, 1962. Apparently the only comprehensive book on this subject, with excellent illustrations.

Wright, Richardson. *The Story of Gardening* (paperback). New York: Dodd Mead, 1934. Authoritative data on the gardens of China, India, Iran and Japan. A classic.

III. ORIENTAL GARDENS IN AMERICA

Better Homes and Gardens.. America's Gardens. New York: Meredith, 1964. Suggestions for home gardeners through color pictures and descriptions of many private and public gardens.

Brooklyn Botanical Garden Record: Handbook of American Gardens. Baltimore: 1970. Handy paperback guide to gardens in the USA, Canada and the Virgin Islands, with emphasis on botanical gardens. Lists their specialties and best seasons. Photographs.

Calkins, Carroll C. *Great Gardens of America.* New York: Coward-McCann, 1969. Descriptions of thirty-five outstanding gardens with fine photographs.

Coates, Peter. *Great Gardens of the Western World.* New York: Putnam's, 1963. Includes description, history and superb photographs of the Japanese garden in San Marino, California.

Doss, Margot Patterson. *Golden Gate Park at your Feet.* San Francisco: Chronicle Books, 1970. Interesting paperback with one chapter about the Japanese Tea Garden. Photographs.

Logan, Harry Britton. *A Traveler's Guide to North American Gardens.* New York: Scribner's, 1974. Lists nearly 1300 gardens including some nurseries and wildflower displays in national parks, in the United States, Puerto Rico,

Virgin Islands and Canada. Also a list of plant societies and state tourist bureaus. Many photographs.

Roberts, Martha McMillan. *Public Gardens and Arboretums of the United States.* New York: Holt, Rinehart & Wilson, 1962. Good descriptions of gardens open to the public in thirty-five states, with excellent photographs.

Cities in which gardens are located.

ALABAMA: Birmingham, Theodore, Tuscaloosa. **ARIZONA:** Carefree. **CALIFORNIA:** Auburn, Culver City, El Cerrito, Glendale, La Canada, Lodi, Los Angeles, Monterey Park, Oakland, Oroville, Pacific Palisades, San Diego, San Francisco, San Jose, San Marino, San Mateo, Saratoga, Whittier. **COLORADO:** Denver. **DISTRICT OF COLUMBIA:** Washington. **FLORIDA:** Delray Beach, Miami, Palm Beach. **HAWAII:** Hilo, Maui, Honolulu, Valley of the Temples, Oahu. **ILLINOIS:** Decatur, Glencoe. **INDIANA:** Michigan City. **LOUISIANA:** Avery Island, New Iberia. **MAINE:** Northeast Harbor. **MARYLAND:** Wheaton. **MASSACHUSSETTS:** Edgartown, Salem. **MICHIGAN:** Saginaw. **MINNESOTA:** Minneapolis. **MISSISSIPPI:** Jackson. **MISSOURI:** Centralia, St. Louis. **NEW JERSEY:** Lakewood, Somerville. **NEW YORK:** Buffalo, Canandaigua, Millbrook, New York City, North Salem. **OHIO:** Akron, Cleveland, Newark, Oberlin. **OKLAHOMA:** Grove. **OREGON:** Portland. **PENNSYLVANIA:** Bethlehem, Malvern, Philadelphia. **RHODE ISLAND:** Providence. **SOUTH CAROLINA:** Sumter. **TENNESSEE:** Memphis, Nashville. **TEXAS:** Austin, Dallas, Fort Worth. **UTAH:** Salt Lake City. **VIRGINIA:** Norfolk, Richmond. **WASHINGTON:** Bellevue, Seattle, Spokane, Tacoma.